The Cat of Port

Maria Strani-

Maria Strani-Potts was born in Corfu, Greece in 1946. She graduated from the School of Slavonic and East European Studies at the University of London. Since 1969 she has travelled widely with her husband, who worked for the British Council. She has lived in Ethiopia, Kenya, England, Greece, Czechoslovakia, Sweden and Australia, where she spent seven years based in Sydney. Maria Strani-Potts divides her time between Corfu and London.

The Cat of Portovecchio

Corfu Tales

Maria Strani-Potts

BRANDL & SCHLESINGER
BOOK PUBLISHERS

All rights reserved. This book is copyright. Apart from any fair dealing for the purposes of study, research, criticism, review, or as otherwise permitted under the Copyright Act, no part may be reproduced or transmitted in any form or by any means, electrical or mechanical, including photocopying, recording, or by any information storage or retrieval system, without permission in writing from the publishers.

The moral right of Maria Strani-Potts to be identified as the author of this work is hereby asserted.

This is a work of fiction. Any resemblance between the characters portrayed and real people, living or otherwise, is purely coincidental.

Copyright © Maria Strani-Potts, 2007

Edited by Diana Giese

First published by Brandl & Schlesinger in 2007
PO Box 127 Blackheath NSW 2785 Australia
www.brandl.com.au

Cover design by Sisi Berati, OK Graphics, Corfu

Book design by András Berkes-Brandl

National Library of Australia Cataloguing-in-Publication entry:

Strani Potts, Maria.
The cat of Portovecchio : Corfu tales.

1st ed.
ISBN 978-1-876040-85-7 (pbk)

I. Title.

823.92

Printed in Australia by Trojan Press

Dedicated to Jim Potts

Acknowledgements

I would like to acknowledge my husband, Jim Potts, who encouraged me like no other. His short poems, quoted at the beginning of many chapters, gave me inspiration. Some of them appear in his collection, *Corfu Blues* (Ars Interpres, Stockholm 2006).

I am also grateful to Dr Judith Black of the Swedish Institute, Stockholm, for her advice and recommendations. Lena Koronaki was my adviser on many Corfiot matters. She is one of my best friends and her opinion and views on the book were of paramount importance to me. Our constructive discussions about 'how things used to be' were precious.

I would like to thank Diana Giese, my editor from Sydney, Australia, for the editing of the book. Her support and advice have been invaluable. Working with her has been a great pleasure. It was a delight to read her almost daily e-mails. They were always encouraging, correct, professional and kind.

I would also like to thank my publishers Veronica Sumegi and András Berkes-Brandl of Brandl & Schlesinger.

The story of *The Cat* is fictional, and so too is Portovecchio.

Corfu (Kerkyra) is real, and has occupied my thoughts every day of my life. If it were not for Corfu, this book would never have been written.

Maria Strani-Potts 2007

Contents

1 A spring death and a drawing room covered in *trahana*
13

2 *Sperna*, fig cakes and two unsuitable marriages
38

3 Portovecchio's sea air fills with the heavenly smell of *frigathelia*, while the priest prepares *savouro*
67

4 A new home, the slaughterhouse, pea stew and *kerkiraiko bourdeto*
85

5 Reminders of an execution, and the procession that brings together innocent souls and sinners
115

6 Morsels of octopus dipped in vinegar assist a fisherman's daughter
145

7 The cat steals, eats and sleeps well, while Joy cooks an inedible *pastitsada*
167

8 Joy comes to the rescue, and trees are uprooted
203

9 Tony's special drink means that Louisa's *balle d'enfants* ends unexpectedly
225

10 Easter midnight soup, and a surprise
258

Food in Portovecchio

Trahana / Soup / Chapter 1
Sperna / Snack / Chapter 2
Sikomaida / Snack / Chapter 2
Frigathelia / Supper / Chapter 3
Savouro / Main meal / Chapter 3
Bizelia yiahni / Main meal / Chapter 4
Bourdeto (fish stew) / Main meal / Chapter 4
Roast chicken and roast potatoes / Main meal / Chapter 5
Agouro-domatosalata / Salad / Chapter 5
Orzo with tomatoes / Light meal / Chapter 6
Boiled prawns and lobster / Main meal / Chapter 6
Octopus dipped in vinegar / Snack / Chapter 6
Marenda / Snack / Chapter 7
Loukoumades / Sweet / Chapter 7
Pastitsada / Main meal / Chapter 7
Sofrito / Main meal / Chapter 8
Tsigareli / Main meal / Chapter 8
Avgolemono / Starter / Chapter 9
Roast turkey with Christmas stuffing / Main meal / Chapter 9
Tony's *tsipouro* / Drink / Chapter 9
Grilled snapper with salad, *halva* and Firiki apples / Main meal / Chapter 10
Yiaprakia / Main meal / Chapter 10
Mayiritsa / Midnight Easter soup / Chapter 10

*Which do you want,
the rats or cats?
Poison the one, you kill the other.*

Chapter 1

A spring death and a drawing room covered in *trahana*

The leaves are not rustling,
The pigeons don't fly–
Wild flowers are saying
'You'll live till you die.'

January–May 1952

Tony was sitting by the window looking out at the blossom on the wild orange trees, from the very back of the dilapidated bus. It was crowded with people going to work. He felt grateful to have found a seat in this suffocating sardine-tin of a city bus. He could no longer take this journey standing and holding the loop which hung from the roof. His destination was an hour away, perhaps more. He had felt exhausted even before getting on; of late his legs had developed a slight trembling when he was standing. A deep fear dominated his thoughts, making his legs feel even weaker and his heart race.

His wife was dying in a grim state hospital at the other end of the city. Tony had learned rather late in life to be thankful for small mercies, so that even this sticky, cracked leather seat at the back of a bus was a welcome gift. Outside, the orange blossom was at its best—white, crisp and pure. It filled the city with its fragrance. The air of Athens was clear, chilly and dry, but inside the bus it was hot and humid. A smell of undigested garlic had settled among the morning passengers. It turned Tony's stomach. He thought hard about the fragrance of the blossom. He wondered if it was only his imagination, a kind of wishful thinking deep inside his brain, but he had trained himself to become expert in mind-over-matter. It didn't always work. The smell of garlic, mixed with a profusion of body odours, formed a repulsive cocktail inside the crowded bus, while the fragrance of the blossom retreated. The stink of garlic could have kept evil, blood pressure and cholesterol well at bay. Even the most saintly and tolerant of Orthodox saints would have run for miles, leaving the passengers to their fate.

Unfortunately for him, Tony was wearing his best grey suit, made of thick English cashmere. He sweated heavily, making him uncomfortably itchy. He knew from experience that the garlicky smell would stick to him for the rest of the day. He never ate it himself, but these daily bus trips had made all his clothes reek forever of garlic. He wondered when it would be possible to take them to the dry cleaners.

The bus was so crowded that many passengers were hanging out of its open doors. It was about eight o'clock in the morning in mid-May 1952 and Tony, on his way to the hospital, was forcing himself to consider the banal notion that it was impossible to predict what lay ahead. He was trying to focus on the idea that nobody ever knows the future. It was possible that the bus might crash and that he would die before his wife, Poppy. This idea frightened him even more. What would then happen to their little daughter, Louisa?

In fact, he knew that God had sentenced Poppy to death. This was certain, as certain as the lack of justice in Greece. Most people were against capital punishment, but executions of Communists were constantly occurring, driving people to despair. Capital punishment was barbaric. Why wasn't God a role model of justice? How could He have sentenced an innocent person such as Poppy so heartlessly to death? She was an innocent, good, loving wife and a tender mother. Both he and Louisa needed her, desperately. At least the Communists executed over the past four years had gone through some sort of judicial process that permitted consideration of their actions or beliefs. Some of them, it was said, had even killed their kith and kin. If he happened to die in some future bus crash, who would look after Louisa? She would be left destitute, the victim of gross injustice. There was no logic in this world.

In spite of this knowledge, a faint hope and illusion kept Tony going. He was praying hard that a *deus ex machina* would change the course of events, that a doctor would call him and say it was all a terrible mistake, and Poppy would get well after all. He was fooling himself, intentionally. He had become a first-class dreamer.

His wife had been sick for months. She was lying in a hospital bed with cancer that had spread throughout her soft, fragile body. Their six-year-old daughter had been installed with his brother and sister-in-law in an apartment to the north of the city. It was not just Tony's emotions that drained him. Circumstances were forcing him to spend endless money on accommodation, medicines, hospital care and city living that he could hardly afford. The hotel where he was staying on his own was third class, but still expensive.

In better times, he had believed that everybody would be healthy forever and that money was there to be spent. He had never curbed his expenses. He had totally failed to respond to the National Bank of Greece's intensive campaign to encourage saving. Every member of his family had enjoyed the very best. Now he was left with his last couple of thousand drachmas in his pocket. He wasn't a religious man, he was a rational man—but he was desperate, and he prayed in spite of his doubts about God, even when he believed that prayer would be useless.

Tony had arrived in this huge city nearly four months earlier, travelling on a boat from his island, bringing with him his six-year-old daughter and his sick wife. Their departure for Athens had taken place soon after Epiphany, when all the family Christmas get-togethers were over, and in the middle of a terrible storm. Luckily it had died down some hours after their departure, as the boat had moved into calmer waters. But the wild storm had upset the little girl, and she complained of stomach pain for the rest of the journey. Tony had to ignore his wife to attend to his daughter, who cried and retched and refused to sleep. Her seasickness had lasted from Kerkyra, or Corfu, to Piraeus, while his wife remained in the cabin's bunk bed for the entire twenty-four hour journey. She, too, was in constant pain, but scarcely ever complained.

They should have departed before Christmas, but Poppy had wanted to spend time at home with all her family. She had refused to believe that she was seriously sick: it was only a bad stomach upset that would go away, she reckoned. 'Let's stay and enjoy Christmas and then we'll see,' she had insisted.

After Christmas her condition had deteriorated. Their family doctor could do nothing to help. 'Take her to Athens,' he had advised.

Tony sold most of the household silver in a hurry. He realised what a fool he had been not to follow the Bank's advice about saving when money was plentiful. All he possessed at the dawn of 1952 was a pile of precious furniture, a lot of antique silver knick-knacks, and his dead sister's jewellery. The desire for aesthetic pleasure had been paramount in his psyche since he was young. He had been an avid collector. He also collected driftwood he found on beaches back on the island. Much good that was to anybody now.

He sold the jewellery, leaving the driftwood to collect dust as it lay on top of his desk in their apartment in Kerkyra.

'Oh God, please give me some indication of what's in store,' he prayed in the back of the bus. Then he shrugged his shoulders at the futility of it all. He thought again of the dry cleaning. He kept gazing at the passing orange trees and remembering a Hummel melody, but that brought uncontrollable tears to his eyes which, in addition to his shaky legs, embarrassed him enormously. Although the bus journey was terribly uncomfortable he still wished it would go on and on and never stop—a continuous trip to eternity.

Tony had married late in life. He had finally found peace, ending years of bachelorhood. Poppy had become his soulmate, the best companion he could possibly have wished for. They had survived the War years together. She was a graceful and intelligent woman, good at her job as a senior civil servant, and kind to all. They both had a passion for Hummel and that was how they had met: they were both members of the Hummel Society. They had become close on a pilgrimage to Bratislava and after they were married, played their favourite Hummel pieces as a duo during winter evenings, he on the mandolin and she on the piano. Although youth had passed for both of them, they managed to produce a little girl, Louisa. Her hair was blonde, almost a pale lemon colour, and her head was heavy with tight, blonde curls. People wondered how it was possible for such a little girl to have so many curls. She always kept her back and head straight so the curls remained static, never succumbing to wind or comb. She was a beautiful child. Her curls made her special, as did her bright blue eyes. They sparkled like Ceylon sapphires in her rosy face. Her glance was like no other. Nobody knew from whom these eyes were inherited. Sometimes her nanny tried to control Louisa's wild hair with ribbons and hats, but to no avail. Everyone spoiled her with toys and entertainment.

Poppy had carried on working after Louisa's birth. Tony was a lawyer. They employed a sensible, strong peasant woman to take care of their daughter. During their afternoon promenades, Louisa and Tina, her nanny, caused quite a stir: the tall nanny dressed in colourful local costume and the little blonde-headed girl in a white organdie dress decorated with appliqué red cherries surrounded with bright green foliage. When the sun was scorching hot a linen hat was inevitably forced on to her head, even though she cried and objected. The hat had a huge brim and was decorated with more bunches of red cherries. It squashed her curls, which had to be fluffed up again when it was taken off.

Things started going wrong when Louisa was five. Poppy started feeling ill. Their doctor couldn't find anything wrong with her. The nanny introduced them to a herbal doctor who recommended endless cups of tea, whose leaves Tony had to go and collect on the nearby mountain. But they had no effect. Poppy stopped working and eating, got thinner by the day, and started spending more and more time in bed. A sad aura of sickness shrouded their apartment. A year later, when bleeding appeared, the doctor said that a trip to Athens was a necessity. When they left for the big city together, nobody knew how long their stay would last. Tony closed his chambers, and they sent the nanny back to her village.

In Athens Poppy was getting worse by the day. Each evening Tony had to visit Louisa and reassure her that everything was fine. She knew exactly what was going on but nevertheless was always jumping about, singing and dancing, showing off, pretending that she couldn't care less. She never asked questions. She hated pity and sour looks. She was too young to express her true feelings, which were unconsciously driving her to the depths of despair. She craved for a happy-go-lucky atmosphere, where people laughed and joked, ate and drank and were merry, just as Tony craved for a glimpse into the future.

Once he had taken Louisa to see her mother. It was so painful that the meeting was cut short, since everybody started weeping. He had swiftly taken Louisa back to his brother's apartment and asked his sister-in-law, Camilla, to take her to the park so she could forget her ordeal. Louisa pretended that the diversion worked. Adopting her jumping-singing way of going about things, she followed her aunt to the little park across the road from the apartment.

Louisa also forced herself to tolerate her Aunt Camilla, in spite of her ridiculous funny-sounding name, which in Greek means *camel*. How could you call out *'Aunt Camilla'* in a park full of children who would burst out laughing every time you used the name? It was also impossible for Camilla to act as a surrogate mother. She had no natural tenderness for humans. She never took Louisa in her arms; she never stroked her hair. Kissing a child was unnatural for her. Her own parents' lack of demonstrative love was what Camilla knew and thought normal.

Camilla was English. What else could she be with such a silly name! She had married Tony's brother soon after they had met in a courthouse in Athens. Max was a prominent Greek barrister who offered his services for free, *pro bono*, to the Hellenic Animal Protection Society. Camilla had met Max when the Society had been taken to court by the state for the hundredth time; again they had illegally dismissed another local vet. She had been representing the British membership of the animal charity, which was a rudimentary local endeavour to save the starving strays of this 'backward country'.

After the first passion of their union had passed, Max came to believe Camilla had been born with an invisible veil of barbed wire around her.

It's often said that young children such as Louisa, in spite of having an enormous sense of their own helplessness, develop a chameleon's ability to adjust. They are stronger than anyone thinks. They are heroic fighters. Unfortunately for them and for the world at large they are not necessarily survivors. In their eyes, adults are always their rock. Adults are necessities: they provide. The absence of an adult sends such children into the depths of despair. But even then an inner strength keeps them afloat, and they hang on to whoever is around. Natural preferences are suppressed, but smiles are not wiped from their faces. They carry on playing and pretending, perhaps for the rest of their lives. Camilla filled the vacuum for Louisa for the time being, as did many others in later years. But she never filled the gaping emotional hole that Poppy's death was to create for the little girl.

In spite of her untouchable air, Camilla was pleasant enough. She provided Louisa with food and a cheerful home, a place where emotions were kept down, nothing sad or depressing was ever discussed, and life went on as 'normal'. At the same time, Camilla devoted herself to her animals. The British members of the Hellenic Animal Protection Society tried extremely hard to teach the Greeks how to treat their animals, especially their cats. They were in the habit of hiring and firing the personnel of the Stray Animals' Unit as easily as the various animals were put to sleep. They had sent Camilla to court to see what was going on, since most of the funding collected in Britain went to pay for lost cases in the Hellenic Court of Justice, instead of for animal welfare. This was not a reflection on Max's professionalism in representing the members, but it could have been, since he was never paid for the services he rendered.

He had offered his services free of charge to the Society not because he was interested in or loved animals, but because he wanted to be invited as often as possible by the British Ambassador to receptions at the grand British residence, in his capacity as the official Legal Adviser of the Hellenic Animal Protection Society. Compared to Tony, with his innate modesty, Max's knowledge of foreign languages had given him highfalutin' ideas on social advancement. His involvement with the Society carried enormous *kudos* in Athenian society. For his part, the British Ambassador was grateful to the animal lovers of Athens, whom he treated as the top-notch socialites of the capital. They provided him with a long list of names for his guest lists. Such lists consisted exclusively of animal lovers, since nobody else in Athens liked the British.

Through her love of cats, Camilla found herself enthroned in a handsome apartment in the northern suburbs of the capital, and heavily involved with the Society. She was absolutely forbidden by Max, however, to keep more than one cat in their home. This animal had been imported all the way from Britain.

After her marriage Camilla started spending a considerable part of her time at the Stray Animals' Unit, talking to the cats before they died. She never entertained the proposition that the cats and other resident animals might understand only Greek. Camilla assumed that the English language was inbred genetically in everybody, humans and animals alike. Since her arrival in Greece she had learned enough Greek to survive, and could have learned more but for her insistence, every time she opened her mouth, on uttering everything in English. When she went out shopping, she addressed the illiterate open-market vendors in English with the self-confidence of someone shopping in Harrods. In the beginning they regarded her with astonishment but slowly, slowly they trained themselves to understand what she wanted. They served her, but considered her rather stupid and backward. When she found herself among her husband's Greek friends she insisted on speaking and expressing herself *through* her husband. This was terribly tiring for him and his friends, but they put up with it out of a strong sense of *philoxenia,* hospitality.

While Poppy was in hospital Camilla agreed to take care of Louisa out of pity and a sense of family obligation. She had no children of her own and no idea how to handle the little girl. She didn't hesitate for a second to leave her with the maid for hours on end, while she spent her time talking to the cats.

Camilla was from Somerset, born and raised in a large manor house, and with animal connections throughout the county. She had a turned-up nose and a scarf was always tied around her straight mousey hair. She gave the impression that she'd gone missing from a gymkhana somewhere in the depths of the English countryside. Her other passion apart from animals was cooking. She talked to the first and wrote about the second. She deeply hoped that one day her cookery books would be bestsellers in every bookshop in Britain and that, with the proceeds, she would be able to save the entire Hellenic animal kingdom.

Camilla loved Max in her own way, but it was obvious that she looked down on his provincial lawyer brother and his family. She had an imperious manner, and in spite of her amiable approach, deep inside she never stopped seeing her Hellenic family as the embarrassing *other*. Tony's family had never visited her in the pre-sickness days. On the contrary, it was always Camilla and Max who travelled to Kerkyra for their annual summer holidays, and benefited enormously from Tony and Poppy's hospitality. Camilla accepted hospitality with flair and many a *thank-you*, but she never reciprocated in kind or emotionally. This time, Max had put his foot down. He called it 'payback time'.

Throughout their years of marriage, Camilla never talked about or introduced her Hellenic family to her relations in England. Greece for her meant handsome Max, animals, food and being on intimate terms with the wives of serving British Ambassadors. It was in this milieu that Louisa found herself on the eve of her mother's death.

At long last, Tony's bus trip came to its end. Heavy-hearted, he dragged himself out of the crowded vehicle into the freshly-scented air. He took a deep breath and lifted his head to stare at the massive white hospital building in front of him. On the roof was a white flag which bore the green emblem of Hippocrates. It flapped at the whim of the wind.

He entered through the hospital's swing doors with a sense of apprehension. He stopped at the little flower shop by the reception desk and bought a bunch of cheap white daisies. During Poppy's illness, he had spent a considerable amount of money at the same shop, buying expensive gardenias which all ended up on the hospital's rubbish heap. The girl wrapped the flowers in paper. He took them without a smile, entered the lift and went up to the fifth floor.

When he got out, he walked down the corridor to her room. He opened the door, and saw two doctors and a nurse standing over Poppy's bed. He did not need to hear what they had to say. He threw the flowers on to an empty chair and asked in a soft voice:

'Has she died?'

Both doctors turned their heads towards him, but the nurse carried on doing something to Poppy. 'Yes, just now. We're so sorry–it was inevitable.' They pulled their stethoscopes from around their necks, placed them in their pockets and one added in a solemn voice:

'We'll be in our office if you'd like to talk to us.' Then they walked out, followed by the nurse who on the way touched his arm lightly.

Tony was left standing looking at Poppy lying on her deathbed. She was still and pale, with her hair loose and her face slightly turned towards him. The nurse had closed her eyes. He looked at her exposed white neck. Should it have looked different in death? He stared at her neck, which was as beautiful and smooth as the first day he had met her.

He felt frozen. He couldn't think about Poppy and her departure. Instead, he thought unwittingly about himself and the years ahead with his little girl. He stood motionless, gazing down at his wife. Then he turned to the chair where he'd deposited the daisies, picked them up and threw them on the floor. He pushed the chair up to Poppy's bed and sat down. The window was open and he could clearly hear the twittering and chittering of the swallows. Spring was at its height, yet Poppy, lying in front of him, had gone forever. The trees would bloom and the birds would sing year after year, and yet this lovely woman had vanished, never to be seen again.

Suddenly Tony felt profound grief, and bitter tears started rolling down his cheeks. He took Poppy's soft hand between his palms and, holding it tightly, he kissed it. She was still warm, and looked relaxed. Then he rested his tired head on her breast. He had no idea how long he stayed there. When he lifted his head, the sun was shining bright and warm through the window. Some wisteria blossom, thick as bunches of purple grapes, was hanging from the balcony above, swaying in the wind, releasing fragrance that entered Poppy's room and gently settled over her body.

A different nurse entered quietly. She had arrived to prepare Poppy for the hospital mortuary. She urged him to leave. He had no reason or strength to resist. Thinking of Louisa, he walked quickly out of the room, his head bent, refusing to look back.

He left the hospital and returned to the bus stop. People were waiting to return to the city. Nobody suspected that Tony was a man whose life had just been destroyed. He wiped the tears from his face. It had turned gloomy and dark and would remain so for the rest of his life.

He had to change buses twice in order to reach his brother's apartment. It was nearly four o'clock in the afternoon when he entered the block. He walked slowly upstairs and rang the bell. Camilla opened the door, holding her precious little black-and-white cat. Louisa was right behind her, cradling a worn-out rag doll. He greeted them both gruffly and walked in.

'How's Poppy today?' Camilla asked indifferently, in English. She did not suspect for a moment that a human life had just come to an end. In fact, she had been preoccupied for the whole day with the end of another life: a dog's. He was a very expensive German shepherd.

That morning she had been called urgently to the Stray Animals' Unit. The guard, a little man who was rather slow mentally, had been very anxious when he phoned her. A foreign couple had deposited a wild beast of a dog a couple of days earlier, he had told her. They had just turned up at the shelter again and wanted something. A foreign tongue was pouring out of their mouths: *'Blah blah blah…'* he imitated them. 'Who knows what they want? Come quickly,' he'd said angrily down the phone.

Only dogs, cats and donkeys could make Camilla run out of her house so speedily. She hadn't once visited Poppy in the hospital and had no intention of doing so. Her excuse was that she respected Tony and Poppy's privacy. How decent can one be?

Tony always wondered about Camilla's reactions, and how much of her character was genetically determined and how much defined by national traits. He always felt a wall of solid ice every time he met somebody from Britain. He was astonished by British people's isolated lives, and their inability to feel comfortable in others' presence. There was a certain aloofness that characterised all social classes. There seemed to be almost no contact between people, unless as a result of persistent effort. They were all continuously stroking some animal or other and only half-listened to what other humans had to say.

Once while walking with Camilla on the Downs outside Bristol, Tony had seen a woman sitting on a bench on her own, weeping profusely. Tony had wanted to approach her and comfort her, to find out what was causing her pain. Camilla angrily stopped him short. 'You do not interfere in other people's lives,' she snapped. 'It's not done in this country. Mind your own business.'

Tony had come to the conclusion that the British were the strangest people in the world. While they disapproved of interfering in each other's lives, they took great pleasure in involving themselves in everybody else's affairs around the world. Take Cyprus, for example. What the Hell were they doing there? He always tried hard to suppress his political thoughts for the sake of his brother. Max was such a strong Anglophile. He had seen his connection with Britain not only as the ticket to the upper classes of Athens, but also as a way of enhancing his professional network.

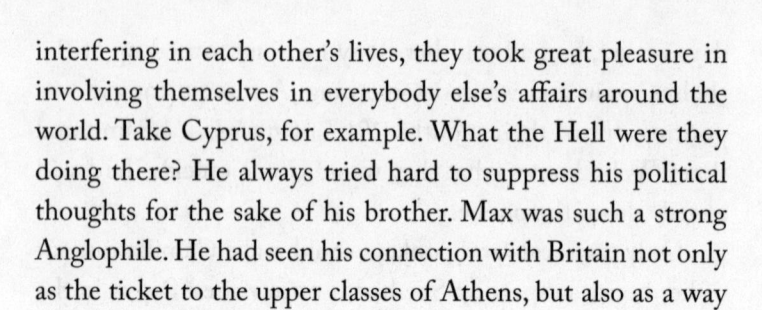

Tony had never really liked Camilla. He disliked her indifference towards Poppy and hated her interference with the Greek authorities over Greek animals. Usually he disguised how he felt. But now he felt so broken that only his resentment could surface.

Camilla was still preoccupied with the incident at the Stray Animals' Unit. After the guard had called, she had arrived there swiftly and short of breath, anxious to find out exactly what was wrong. She had a pretty good idea, however, of what had happened. Similar incidents took place regularly with foreigners.

On entering the smelly unit she had come face to face with an agitated British couple. They were cursing and shouting at the guard in disagreeable Cockney accents. He looked lost and puzzled.

'What's going on?' Camilla asked as civilly as she could. 'Our bloody dog—we want our dog! We want to pay for the two-day stay, take him and go. This bloody idiot won't give us our dog. He doesn't speak a word of English.'

All this came out in one breath and almost, but not quite, in a chorus that involved both. The expectation that humans and animals alike ought naturally to speak English was all too evident. Both the man and the woman were dressed in tweeds and sandals. Their toes, crowned with dirty nails, were sticking out like hostile frogs.

'What dog? Where did you leave your dog?' Camilla asked in her county accent, pushing her turned-up nose higher. She had taken an immediate dislike to her compatriots. Greeks always embarrassed Camilla, but she also detested anybody living beyond the borders of Somerset. Her manner aggravated the couple even more. Although both sides obviously loved animals, Camilla had a deep conviction that Londoners like these two were unworthy of possessing any kind of animal. Londoners were a different breed, and Camilla was convinced that they undermined the essence of Englishness.

'We arrived from Patras very late, two nights ago. We had no idea where the camp sites were in this bloody city, so we had to go and find somewhere to sleep. In the hotel they refused to let us have Nigger with us in our room, and they directed us to these kennels. They said we could leave him here and somebody would take care of him. This idiot took him in, and now he pretends he doesn't know us. He won't give us our dog back!'

Camilla remembered that the guard had informed her that the last entry to the unit had been a huge dog, deposited by some foreigners. Ignorant as he was, he had no idea what kind of breed any dog was, nor indeed that there was such a thing as a precious pedigree. In his mind all dogs were mongrels or strays destined to be put to sleep. The new Animal Protection Society vet had visited earlier that morning. His job was to put all the previous days' strays to sleep—which he had done.

Camilla turned to the guard: 'Did they bring you a dog two days ago?' she asked in order to confirm the claim, and to show that she was at least helping by translating. Then when he nodded, she turned to the Cockney couple in disdain, taking the side of the guard, maybe for the first time ever. 'Don't you realise that this poor man doesn't speak English?' she enquired arrogantly. 'He's Greek, you know.' She really was angry. Cockneys were totally out of place in Greece.

The guard interrupted her by shouting: 'Yes, they did bring in this horrible-looking beast, and the vet sorted him out this morning. I've already put him in the oven.'

'Oh, my God,' Camilla thought. She turned immediately and furiously to the couple:

'Didn't you realise that this is a Stray Animals' Unit, my dears? These are not kennels.'

She had adopted her most patronising and angry tone to prove that she was in the right and they were in the wrong. Then she looked for the first time at the little receipt that they had handed her. It was a standard note in Greek given when they had deposited their dog, a standard courtesy thank-you note from the Animal Protection Society. It was thanking them for their effort in saving a stray dog from a miserable life on the streets of Athens.

'Your dog has been put to sleep. Obviously it's all been a terrible mistake,' she told them. 'You'd better leave now.' All this was conveyed in her hard, upper-class voice.

The Cockney woman had started weeping, while the man cursed and threatened legal action. Camilla more or less pushed them out of the shelter and ordered the guard to lock the place up for the day. They hurried towards their car, yelling and threatening them.

When Tony had arrived at her apartment, Camilla was still stressed. The death of the dog had upset her. She was trying hard to find comfort by stroking her cat, which nestled safe and sound in her arms.

Her enquiry in English about Poppy had annoyed Tony. Given the state he was in, he found it impossible to react in a foreign language. He had come to announce a mother's death to a six-year-old child who was now looking at him with a welcoming, smiling face and two brilliant Ceylon-sapphire eyes.

'Would you like some tea?' Camilla continued in English, ignoring his angry silence. He had to force himself to answer. 'No,' he responded, drily, in Greek. Anger beyond his control had started welling up inside him. This ridiculous stupid battle-axe of a woman never understood that Greeks drank tea only when they had a bad stomach. For Louisa's sake, he kept calm, hiding his devastation, pain and anger. He lightly kissed her blonde head and took her by the hand. Then he opened the door of the drawing room and entered, pulling little Louisa behind him, leaving Camilla standing in the entrance hall.

He wanted to be on his own with his little girl, to explain. He couldn't utter a word in front of this alien woman stroking a pathetic cat with such affection.

He was quite unprepared for what happened next. Suddenly, in a totally non-British way, Camilla screamed: 'Oh, please come out of there, *please*. My *trahana* has been laid out in there to dry. Shut the door!'

But Tony and Louisa had already entered the grand drawing room, an extremely successful transplant from the days of colonial Britain. The furniture consisted of expensive

English antiques that Camilla had inherited from her distinguished family. The paintings on the walls had come from her family's estate in Scotland, and the carpets which covered the well-polished floor had been brought from India by male forebears who had worked for the East India Company. Today, however, there was something extraordinary about the room. Momentarily forgetting his plight, Tony, tightly holding Louisa's hand, took two steps back.

The drawing room was covered from wall to wall with a white grain-like substance. The windows were closed, but the shutters were open, letting the light filter in through the glass, to warm this snow-white carpet that covered the floor, the tables, the chairs and the sideboard. Camilla had placed big stainless steel trays lined with tea towels throughout the elegant drawing room. On top of the starched white pieces of cloth she had spread her *trahana*.

Camilla had spent hours during her last holidays in Central Zagori talking to a Sarakatsanissa from the semi-nomadic Sarakatsani tribe of Epirot livestock-breeders. This woman possessed four hundred adorable goats and three hundred cuddly sheep, and specialised in dairy by-products. She had given Camilla her supposedly secret recipe for *trahana*, a kind of Greek soup pasta. Camilla had written it down in her poor Greek and it had taken her nearly a year to transcribe it into perfect English. The recipe had been given in confidence; little did its owner know that Camilla planned to include it in her intended bestselling cookbook.

While Camilla looked down on Greece, its food was another matter. She had loved *trahana* soup from the beginning, and was eager to learn how to prepare it herself. The woman in the Zagori had told her it was necessary for freshly-made *trahana* to be spread over a large area to dry, for five to eight days. The only large area Camilla had was her elegant drawing room. Usually the cat was allowed to roam there freely, but for the last eight days the adorable Jack had been restricted to the rest of the house.

Since obtaining the recipe, Camilla had made many attempts to make *trahana*, but because she was too proud to ask linguistic questions about the recipe she got it wrong time and time again. Finally she got the *trahana* more or less right, and her recipe into perfect English. Years later the recipe was still in her kitchen drawer, unpublished, dirty and torn, a fate similar to that of her marriage.

Now she was screaming: 'This apartment isn't mine any more! You come and go as you please. I look after Louisa, fine, but do you have to come here so often? Can't you stay in the hospital, or at the hotel a bit more? My poor Jack gets so disturbed with all these comings and goings.' She was beside herself. She'd had such a dreadful day, what with the dog and now with Tony turning up uninvited and opening the door of the drawing room, exposing all her lovely *trahana*.

The noise she was making stopped Tony and Louisa from going any further. But it also made Jack the cat jump from Camilla's arms towards where Louisa was standing. Jack and Louisa had developed a warm and loving relationship. Louisa adored him, cuddled him and treated him like her baby. The cat's black-and-white coat with its softness and warmth had become a kind of substitute for her mother's bosom.

Jack stopped only momentarily at Louisa's feet and then ran on into his favourite drawing room. Immediately he started jumping with gusto all over the *trahana*. At once the drawing room was transformed into a mini-snowfield.

Camilla went on screaming in English. Louisa laughed with all her heart and started chasing the cat around the room. Tony froze. He was anxious, devastated; his very soul felt empty. He could see that he had lost the precious moment to explain to his little girl about her mother.

Dejectedly he left, banging the door behind him, cursing Camilla and the cat.

With the passing of time, besotted Max became fed up with cats, bad quality *trahana* and the nuances of the English language. A few years after Poppy's death, Camilla was sent packing. Unfortunately for her, she couldn't afford to return to cheerful Somerset where adorable cats were the norm. She just managed to buy a semi-detached house on the outskirts of Bridport in Dorset, where she spent the rest of her life protecting families of foxes. Her ambition to write a bestseller evaporated along with her Greek marriage.

For the first time in his life Max fell deeply in love, with a sophisticated and elegant town-dwelling Sarakatsanissa lawyer. After his divorce from Camilla, they married. Elleni's recipe for *trahana* never suffered the perils of poor translation and was always made with pure ingredients straight from the sheepfold, in August when milk was plentiful. Elleni would leave her practice in Athens and spend that month in the Zagori. Once there, she would mix five pints of yoghurt with a tablespoon of salt and lots of plain flour, to make stiff dough.

Then she made little balls from the dough, the size of ping-pong balls. With her ancient rolling pin she patted them flat and spread them on white kitchen towels to dry. When dry she crumbled them into thousands of pieces and let them dry some more.

Elleni never had to put them out to dry in her Athens sitting room. She always made her *trahana* during their summer holidays up in the Zagori. She would spread it out on tables in the yard, covered with muslin cloths. After five days the *trahana* was always ready to be packed in airtight jars. She used it in the winter months, making it into soup with beef stock, tomato paste, butter and crumbled feta. She served it to Max warm and free of cat's hair, accompanied with plenty of uncomplicated mountain-style love. This made him grateful for Camilla's departure and for Elleni's arrival.

The British Ambassador, of course, never gave up on Max. He carried on inviting him, since the list of the friends of Britain was becoming shorter and shorter because of the Cyprus situation. Anybody prepared to put his snobbery and love for animals above honest patriotism was more than welcome at the British Ambassador's residence.

In the end, the Animal Protection Society, failing to change the fate of Hellenic animals, closed down. It was encumbered with debts and pursued by lawyers.

Poppy's family wanted Tony to take her body back to the island. He refused, for two reasons: the first financial and the second his inability to explain to Louisa what had happened.

He decided to bury his wife, her mother, without telling her. Poppy was put to rest in a cemetery in the big city. Tony was relieved, since he had no strength left to make the trip back on the boat with her in her coffin. He was almost penniless, with just enough money to return home with his daughter. But he made a promise over Poppy's coffin that in three years' time, when his finances had recovered, he would return, exhume her and take her bones back to the family grave on the island.

Poppy's family was furious. But by the time they had offered to pay the costs of transportation, she had been buried.

With empty pockets, a broken heart and a little girl in tow, Tony returned to the island.

He kept Poppy's death a secret from Louisa for nearly three years. He was furious with Camilla and her indifference. He had lost forever the moment when he could have opened his heart to his little girl and explained in an honest and straightforward way what had happened. He pretended that Poppy was still alive and getting better in the city, and that one day she would come back. He never mentioned her mother's name again to Louisa, never talked about her or their life together. He was not fooling her, but himself.

For three years he mourned her with a black band round his sleeve. He would take it off in Louisa's presence. His finances never improved. As a widowed lawyer of over fifty he found it difficult to pick up the pieces of his business. At the end of the three years he borrowed some money from a friend, secretly left for Athens, and had his Poppy exhumed. Her bones were put in a tin box and illegally transferred back to Kerkyra in his suitcase.

He never had the strength of will to bury her in the cemetery. Instead he placed her tin box in a deep hole in the back yard of his chambers. He never told anybody about the transfer. He always meant to, but he kept procrastinating. Poppy lay buried in the yard forever after.

Tony took his secret to his own grave in the grand family tomb. The rusty and decaying tin with Poppy's broken bones is still under the courtyard of a smart, modern glass-fronted building of some new legal chambers. The bulldozer missed it by a metre when the ground was being excavated. Nowadays, above that tin box, young barristers relaxing in the courtyard smoke a cigarette or drink their take-away coffee in the shade of a purple-mauve wisteria which is nearly fifty years old.

Chapter 2

Sperna, fig cakes and two unsuitable marriages

*The wine that once spoke has turned bitter.
Bread soaked in sour wine
Our autumn rations.*

Autumn 1955

Autumnal storms are spectacular in Kerkyra. They start with a mild, refreshing wind, which is welcomed by everyone in the humid heat of the season. Slowly and steadily they build momentum. First the sky turns a pale silver-grey, then it deepens and darkens. The branches of the trees sway and the open window shutters start banging. At any moment they might come unhinged. This seldom happens–at least not because of the storms.

Once, in the autumn of 1943, the shutters and the buildings to which they were attached did–literally–crash to the ground. For ten days the Germans bombarded the island. They caused such extensive damage and devastation that it took years to put everything right. Where the old buildings once stood open craters formed, filled with their own sad ruins of dirt and rubble. Pepper trees grew and blossomed, and children played hide-and-seek there. The inhabitants still lament this senseless destruction and hate Nazi Germany and Fascist Italy for causing it.

Like other places in the world, the Old Town of Kerkyra didn't escape the ravages of World War II, yet some elements of its ancient Venetian style remain, and are resilient in the face of all weathers. Ferocious storms, regular earthquakes, blistering sun and damp heat, even snow have failed to spoil this magical little town. The buildings that the War didn't touch, buildings as old as the history of Europe, still stand tall and brave.

Unfortunately, nobody spends money or time on maintaining them. There have always been other priorities. In countries where health and education are luxury commodities, who will plan the careful redecoration of a building that can't really suffer from the lack of social services? Three, four and five-storey houses appear wobbly and hazardous, with the odd tile or brick hanging precariously. But since nobody's head has been crushed by a falling tile, and since the cost of maintaining these buildings is otherwise minimal, people aren't at all anxious about them. If anything, the old buildings are regarded like precious, if often neglected members of a large extended family. They're loved more from the outside; they feel less comfortable and are less tolerated from the inside.

On the whole, the inhabitants of Kerkyra hate spending time indoors. They see no point in it. Instead, they make full use of the elegant town squares that act as lavish communal sitting rooms. There the servants—that is, the waiters—carry trays of delicacies back and forth. People can stretch out and read the newspapers, hear all the gossip and see their acquaintances casually, without any obligations or long-term commitments to reciprocal hospitality, and without having to clean or tidy up afterwards.

The café armchairs in the squares are the best and most effective psychiatrists' couches the world has to offer. Under the shade of the lime trees family problems tend to find their solutions. For hours on end hardships are discussed among friends until they have spilled right out, leaving everyone's chests lighter and happier. Thanks to such philosophical discussions, and with the aid of strong coffee, double ouzos, freshly squeezed orange juice and much more, problems come to seem trivial. They can often become the subject of jokes. Houses are merely places to sleep in; places where one can have a bath or go to the lavatory; places to protect the occupants from the darkness of the night and the bad moods of the weather; places in which to make love in private or where possessions can be stored.

The buildings of Kerkyra remain unrepaired, unpainted, rickety, flaking, but still charming and precious. Everybody looks at them with adoration and the only time they turn their backs and run away in fear is when the giant *Enceladus* struggles to break out, shaking the island mercilessly. When *Aeolus* blows with all his might, with or without torrents of grey rain, everyone runs to find shelter under the arches of the buildings, laughing and enjoying the experience. They know that the island will not sink into the depths of the Ionian Sea.

In September, winds arrive with graceful might. The café armchairs and the sun umbrellas blow away. The trees have no choice but to turn and bow in the direction in which the strong, warm winds are forcing them. Sometimes the trees break and collapse, unable to resist the insistent power of the winds. Lightning flashes in the sky; there are bombardments of thunder. The drinking of coffee, ouzo and orange juice is disrupted; drivers are afraid that the wind and rain will blow their cars off course, yet they carry on with their journeys.

These downpours are not just heavy rain. Billions of leaves also fall from the trees, not all of them autumnal copper-yellow. Many are still green and fresh, since autumn always arrives suddenly. There is no time for a slow metamorphosis. Children scream among them and adults run to protect their sons and daughters. Such commotion generates as much energy as the wind which creates it. Then the rain falls fast, heavy and thick. The storms are not tropical, but they are similar and often worse. Their force seems to thrust in from all directions. The blue sea turns a dark frothy grey.

Ferries remain tied up in the disturbed harbour as business slows down. Every year the municipality is taken by surprise and is unprepared. Half the drains are blocked with leaves and rubbish. The other half have been blocked intentionally. During the summer, pieces of cardboard are placed tightly on top of these square holes, to stop the distinctive smell of Kerkyra's drains from escaping into the streets. The town always floods.

Nobody minds; every year it's the same. Bored by the endless hours of summer swimming, the island's people welcome the new season. A change of routine invigorates them; it gives new direction to their interests and makes them less lethargic.

At the time of the first storms, the schools re-open. Children, some more eager than others, turn up with new schoolbags.

The swallows have not yet flown south, and the cheese-pie sellers are looking forward to providing plenty of snacks at breaks, to boost their meagre incomes.

The storms last four days at the most. Then summer reappears. It is hot, humid and wonderful again. The cicadas become noisier than ever. The swallows shriek louder. The empty beaches are slowly invaded again. The sea, gleaming in the orange sun, becomes light blue and lukewarm, making swimmers feel completely comfortable and secure. They do not swim purposefully as in the summer months; they just take dips and float, looking up and around in awe at the tall, pinkish, rocky mountains. It seems as if Albania could be reached just by stretching out a hand.

The Lord of Creation has been extravagantly generous to Kerkyra—but we in return have been most ungrateful to Him.

Weather conditions and cheese-pie selling were, are and will be much the same for years to come, but this year's autumnal storm was different for Blossom. She married during a storm. As a thunderbolt struck, shaking the church, she uttered the irrevocable 'yes'. She would have preferred kinder weather, perhaps not as hot, since she loathed the heat, which made her perspire profusely. On the way to the church her white silk suit got terribly muddy around the hemline, and some flowers she'd placed on her short, thick, curly hair were blown away by the wind. At the ceremony, her hair flying loose in disarray, she looked as if she'd just been electrocuted. She was left with no redeeming decorative feature for her untidy head and face except a forced smile.

Blossom had mixed feelings about this enormous change in middle life. But she had prayed hard it would be for the best.

All her life she'd been told what to do and this latest move was also being made under the influence of a gentle command.

So far it had been impossible for Blossom, now well into her forties, to find somebody willing to marry her. This was not only because of her lack of height and generous weight; most of all, it had to do with her bow-legs. When she stood up or walked a great O was formed below her hem. Only a long skirt could have covered them. Unfortunately, such skirts were not in fashion.

There were a few other reasons, too, why Blossom had remained a virgin into middle age. Her wiry hair, her bulging dark brown eyes, her flat nose and thick lips wouldn't attract any man, regardless of his own looks. A prospective husband couldn't have known, when he saw her for the first time, of her kindness, her expertise in cooking, sewing and embroidery, and her ability to withstand hardship and harsh treatment. All the men in her village took one look at her and ran away. The male population had the power of making the choice, of doing the picking; the female population was there to be picked. Women had to wait like fruit on a tree for somebody to come by, take a fancy to them, pluck them and gobble them up. Then after the man had taken the first bite he would decide whether the fruit was to his satisfaction. The fruit could never complain about the sharpness of male teeth. It was unfortunate that the fruit couldn't turn itself, by magic, into a hard beach pebble to make the man's rotten teeth crumble into little pieces.

Blossom, like any other fruit, had been waiting and waiting, ripening by the minute. If she were not picked soon she was in danger of rotting.

Blossom could offer one substantial advantage. This had been well advertised by her brother, who was desperate to marry her off. She had quite a bit of money to her name. Her family had gained considerable experience from the difficulties they had encountered in marrying off her two ugly sisters. They were prepared to allocate Blossom a handsome dowry. Couldn't somebody at least marry her for her money?

Blossom had graduated very successfully from primary school but had not advanced further in letters; this was not unusual in the 1950s for women from the countryside. Her wider education had been of a high standard. Domestic science, taught at home, had given her invaluable knowledge. Her expertise was renowned in the area, and women from all around used to visit her and seek her advice. She never cooked professionally, but she did produce exquisite embroidery for others, who paid well for her services. When somebody from the island was getting married the entire trousseau was embroidered, crocheted and knitted by Blossom and by the helpers she would employ.

And she had even more skills. When consulted, she gave acquaintances ideas for menus for weddings, funerals, engagements, christenings and name-day parties. She never charged for her oral advice, but she did make quite a lot of money from her needlework. She was too compassionate to profit much from it, but she got a great deal of pleasure from hiding her little income in a big round chocolate box. When the pile of paper money interfered with the tight fit of the lid, she took the money out, went to town and deposited it in the bank.

On Saint Barbara's day each December, she would rise before the winter sun, go into the dark kitchen and light the oil lamps. Then, with all the confidence of a French chef she would produce the most wonderful *sperna* in the district. For Blossom this was the highlight of her cooking diary. She loved preparing them, and she loved eating them. She would take whole-grain wheat and soak it for three days, rinsing it many times with fresh water, and then would boil it for as long as it took to become soft but not mushy, like whole grains of cooked rice. She then drained the wheat through a sieve and again through another sieve which had been lined with muslin. She left it there for an hour to drain completely, and then placed it in a big clay pot. She would already have prepared the little red juicy pearls of two pomegranates, handfuls of sultanas and currants, and washed and dried almonds. The almonds would have been shelled and had their skins removed by plunging them in boiling water for a few minutes. She would add them with lots of aniseed and chopped walnuts to the wheat. Then she sprinkled over a little ouzo and put in a moderate amount of sugar and plenty of cinnamon. After she'd mixed everything together with a real feeling of joy in her good heart, she placed the *sperna* in big silver-plated dishes and decorated them with chopped crystallised pears, figs and small white sugar-almonds.

When she was finished she placed the platters for a couple of hours on the dining table, where she hovered round and admired them like a sculptor admiring his masterpiece. Then she distributed them to all who came to visit and to pay their respects to her ancient mother, whose name was Barbara.

Eating was one of Blossom's favourite pastimes. No wonder she was ample and round like a huge snowball. When naked, she was a fleshy white ball with plenty of nice soft folds. When clothed, she was drab and colourless. Perhaps her legs were bent because they were too short to carry the weight of her body.

The combination of needlework and good cooking are deadly for a woman, unless accompanied by vigorous exercise. Women then never considered such a thing, and Blossom obviously did not exert herself physically. Because of their solid economic status, her family did not have to send their women to the fields. Her face, on which she wore a permanent sweet smile, remained white and smooth as a baby's bottom. The scorching Mediterranean sun hadn't had many encounters with her, and when it did, she was well covered with appropriate clothing and kerchiefs.

Most of the time Blossom stayed indoors. She embroidered, cooked and ate.

Her life was good, apart from constant reminders of the need for marriage by her brother and by Elektra, his wife. Blossom was entering marriage with some hesitation, and constant prayers to God to help her. She had always believed that at some point—sooner rather than later—she would have to leave her family home where her brother and his wife had set up residence by traditional right. Blossom knew that the life of a spinster living with a sister-in-law could become as bad as a nightmare.

In the beginning, Elektra had been kind and co-operative. But soon after she married Blossom's brother George she became tense, impatient, snappy, moody and fiercely independent. Her sharp irony hurt many people, but most of all Blossom. She would insult her about her virginity in a cruel, crude manner.

Something had snapped in Elektra and nobody knew what it was. She had bought a dozen chickens, two sheep, a dog and a donkey and spent all her time in the garden looking after them. She never did any housework, leaving the running of the home to Blossom. She never cooked, with one exception. She had a couple of enormous fig trees in her garden. Every summer she spent hours, when the figs were plentiful, making fig cakes, *sikomaida*. It seemed that everything loving in her nature had been diverted towards her animals and the fig trees. When the weather was hot, she sat under them keeping an eye on her animals, which wandered freely in the garden. Occasionally she would pick up a spear of the hard gold grass sprouting from the dry earth where she had come to rest, and with it would pick her teeth, carefully and slowly, back and forth. She had suffered from bad gums since her teens, so this hard massage would cause them to bleed, leaving her mouth rejuvenated and fresh, at least for a little while.

She would look at the sky through the thick foliage of the fig trees and her thoughts would wander through her childless life, which she saw as a domestic prison. She was constantly drowsy because she slept badly. It was as if the gentle breeze moving through her garden sucked out her thoughts and took the weight from her overloaded brain. Soon she would fall asleep in the shade.

Elektra's apron pockets were always full of smooth golden grains of corn with which she used to feed her chickens. She adored them and she'd given them people's names. She knew exactly which was which. The chickens responded to their individual names as if they could understand Greek.

She used to climb her fig trees with the agility of a squirrel. She would sit for a while on the most comfortable branch to rest and eat as many figs as her stomach could take. She would fill the basket she carried with her, climb down from the tree, and go into the kitchen, which she hardly ever frequented. There she would start cooking her *sikomaida* in the most erratic, yet successful way.

She took the figs out of her basket, split them in two and spread them on tin trays in the sun to dry. She covered them with thin muslin so that bees and flies wouldn't get them—but sometimes they did. She didn't care a bit about the flies or the bees. This was the only time that Blossom had the upper hand. She would nag her about her questionable hygiene, so in order to avoid her whining voice, Elektra covered them as best she could. When the figs were dried out, she chopped them up with a big sharp knife and kneaded them with fresh unfermented grape juice and some ouzo, and let them soak a bit to become soft again. After a while she added chopped walnuts, almonds and some aromatic edible gum-resin and then, with great fervour, kneaded them again. She formed little round cakes the size of a big English doughnut, patted them flat and put them in a moderate oven to dry—but just for a short time.

When they were cold she wrapped them up in fig leaves and tied them with string. She stored them in a cupboard and had them ready for when the sorrow of her life became unbearable, and figs were out of season.

Elektra had one more passion: Chinese dates. At the bottom of her garden, a medium-sized date tree, the only one in the village, gave plentiful fruit every year. She would distribute the Chinese dates in handfuls. All the children flocked around, grateful for her generosity. Those that were left she'd dry on her baking trays spread out in the sun.

Her dried dates and her perfect round fig cakes made Elektra very popular. Friends wondered why such a good-looking woman, full of wit and sparkle before her marriage, had become so moody. They decided she must have serious disagreements with her husband. Or perhaps Blossom's constant presence in her home was getting her down. Fancy having to face Blossom wobbling round the house, eating and giggling all day!

Half their gossip was correct. Blossom was part of her problem, but George was the *entire* problem. Elektra had come to detest him and when she wasn't ignoring him, she was rude to him both in private and in public. They never, never did things together.

Marital relationships in those days remained the most confidential matters in the world. Unless one of the partners was desperate enough to let something slip, or a scandal of infidelity exploded in the village, no-one ever came out in the open and said what the problem was. So Elektra's mood remained a mystery. The secret problem was so shameful that neither she nor her husband could utter a word about it. George was impotent. Although he possessed the most enormous testicles, never in his life had he had an erection or even physical desire for a woman.

Elektra had known her husband since they were young children. They had been good friends and playmates in the schoolyard. When he grew up, George never looked at women in a special way. Neither did Elektra go out with anybody. It was their families who arranged the marriage. As was usual in the village, they were not intimate before their wedding. Even holding hands and fleeting kisses were out of bounds.

It was only after a month of marital 'bliss' that Elektra realised that her husband was totally useless. He just couldn't do it. In the beginning she kept asking him, politely, *why not?* Then he would leave the bedroom in a sulk without giving an answer. He'd march into the kitchen, pick up some leftover food and return to the bedroom, munching and unapproachable.

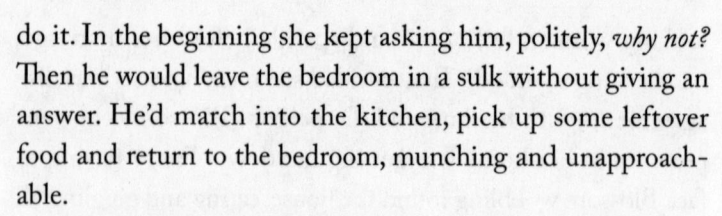

One day, after she had humiliated him with bitter words, Elektra blocked the bedroom door with her body, using her two outstretched arms as a barrier to stop him from leaving. He retreated back into the room and sat down on the end of their perfectly-made bed, looking timid, serious, and sad.

He said in a soft voice, lowering his head: 'It's Blossom.'

'Blossom? What's it got to do with Blossom?' Elektra asked, with surprise.

'I can't behave in *that* way when Blossom's asleep next door. Hopefully she'll marry soon and then the whole house will be just for the two of us. We'll be free to do whatever we like.'

Elektra had believed him, but still couldn't control her anger, hard as she tried. The absence of what she had dreamed of and expected in marriage hit her hard. She took George's rejection as a severe personal insult, and made no allowance for his own embarrassment.

She developed enormous hatred for poor Blossom and impotent George. She wished Blossom out of her way as soon as possible. Blossom, in spite of her spinsterhood, was quite content. If it hadn't been for Elektra, her tranquillity and peace of mind would have sustained her to the end of her life. She was sad, however, that George and Elektra hadn't produced any children. She would have loved to present George with a ready-made baby in a basket herself, the way she had used to give him the best present on New Year's Eve.

Blossom had never fancied nor fallen in love with any man, nor even spared them a thought. All her life George had been the only target of her female tenderness. She loved George's looks, which were like hers. On manly George, however, dark curly hair and bulging eyes were somehow becoming. Blossom and George were two sides of the same coin. As nature would have it, two sides of the same coin can never face one another, yet they are as close as can be.

Blossom's family home had always been her sanctuary. It was Elektra's arrival that forced her to escape into daydreaming. While embroidering, crocheting and knitting she would fantasise about having her own place. She would be able to do whatever she liked there without the constant nagging of another woman. She felt no particular personal resentment towards Elektra, but an uncomfortable feeling had settled deep inside her. Blossom never acknowledged her jealousy, since she couldn't recognise it. She wasn't too bright. The possibility of an utterly miserable marriage never crossed her mind either.

Nor did she question the nature of her feelings towards George. She was too naïve to force herself to distance herself from him for her own good. She was also too innocent to foresee the possibility that a marriage of her own would turn her into a domestic slave. She was about to plunge into this proposed marriage in total ignorance. She had only her dreams, and her obedience to George's pressure. She would live to regret it.

The marriage-broker called on Tony at his chambers, by invitation. Tony received him with embarrassment. He declared, in his barrister's authoritative, gruff tones: 'I need to get married.'

Tony had for some time been thinking of visiting Mr Theofillos, the broker, and asking for his help. But he kept postponing the visit. The thought of his dead wife Poppy had haunted him for nearly three years. His failure to tell Louisa of her death continued to torment him. If he could only bring himself to utter the dreaded words 'Your mother is dead', then perhaps he could take some decisions, and they could both move forwards.

The incident with the cat at Camilla's apartment had seemed to make him lose his reason. The world's indifference to his pain had damaged him severely. He had lost his soulmate, and his desire for human contact had shrunk to what was absolutely necessary. It was sometimes as if he were paralysed.

Since their return from Athens, Tony and Louisa's lives had changed dramatically. As a middle-aged man, Tony was left only with the company of his little girl. In Kerkyra, he had become silent and tended to weep at the smallest of sorrows. It's sometimes said that men don't cry. Tony never *used* to cry, either. Now his eyes were watery most of the time. He kept explaining to anyone who bothered to notice that his tear ducts were infected and that he was on a course of treatment. But he was really still a wreck, lost in grief.

The idea of marrying again came to him while he was sitting under the lime trees in the square, drinking one ouzo after another, always accompanied with a couple of aspirin. His migraines had become impossible, to the point where he was more full of aspirin than regular food. But the more ouzo he consumed to dull the pain, the more the pain increased. Tony felt exhausted, and permanently sick. He could see Death approaching again, this time to take *him*. And then where would Louisa be?

He also suffered from insomnia, which he tried to ignore by endlessly reading novels by Guy de Maupassant. His nightmares during his short spells of sleep took him back and forth to Athens, carrying a gold box which he couldn't unlock. When awake he became obsessed with illness, with Louisa the target of his fears.

He knew he couldn't carry on keeping up with the housework, the cooking, and taking care of his daughter. Most seriously of all, he was in a financial mess–in short he was broke. Since his wife's death, he had been unable to complete any legal case with even moderate success. His mind was all over the place. And attendance at court was during school hours.

Very few people wanted him as a lawyer. He kept a minor position as a legal adviser to a bank, and this guaranteed a minimum income. But he was fed up and tired. Only this morning he'd had to scrub the two flights of stairs up to their apartment, on his own. The maid-cum-nanny had left them. Her wages were overdue. Numerous stray cats came to foul and sometimes even vomit on their staircase. Tony would cover the messes with sand and leave them there for a couple of days to dry. Then he would sweep them into a dustpan and throw them in the dustbin. He put down special powder to deter the cats from returning, but they did, leaving more and more droppings. They were driving him mad. The combination of loneliness, obligations and problems sometimes led him to consider killing himself.

In his better moods, he knew he had to find somebody to do the housework, look after Louisa, clean up after the cats and—most important of all—bring some money into his empty purse. It never crossed his mind that he would need something to offer in return. His once-sharp legal mind had run out of alternative solutions. He had to find a bride. He didn't care who she was or where she was from. What he needed was money. He needed a dowry and an unpaid maid.

The plan to find somebody whirled around his cloudy, ouzo-filled brain like a spinning top. He reckoned that it wouldn't be too difficult. But first of all he had to announce to his daughter that her mother was dead. He still found it impossible to find the correct way to tell her. He couldn't pluck up his courage. He was incapable of uttering the words. As the days passed, he sometimes even forgot that he had never told her. He was afraid that if he said the dreaded words out loud he'd frighten himself to death, that his broken heart would stop from the immense pain he felt.

Tony was surprised and a bit shocked by the sound of his own voice when he declared to the marriage-broker in a loud, clear and confident voice that he wanted to marry. He was astonished that he could make such a declaration to somebody he hardly knew. This was completely out of character.

But nothing shocked the marriage-broker. Mr Theofillos was an ugly, middle-aged man, like most of his clients. He had arrived at Tony's office dressed in a sombre suit and a trilby hat. From his arm hung a mock-Burberry trench coat, folded inside out, so that the Burberry lining was on show to the world. He never wore it unless he was desperate. The trench coat was second-hand and torn. The lining was what mattered. It gave him a touch of class and evoked a feeling of trustworthiness, which he badly needed in his profession.

Mr Theofillos was very good at his job and had an impeccable reputation. He had been in this line of business since the War ended. When he had returned from fighting the Italians and Germans, he had several bullet wounds in his body and not many employment prospects. He had decided on this profession after successfully introducing his sister to an army mate.

He conducted his business in a matter-of-fact way, approaching the marriage negotiations like an estate agent. He organised his files with photos taken in blooming gardens, from a distance. His commission was based on a percentage of the woman's dowry, and his profit was always good, guaranteeing him a healthy income. Men never placed a penny on the bargaining table. The male contribution was no more than a hairy back made generously available to the bride, and an offer to take her on a one-way journey out of the paternal home and into an unknown future. Most of the time the journey was bumpy and uncomfortable, the ride of an inexperienced, overweight rider on a camel's back.

'That's a very good idea,' Mr Theofillos said to Tony, looking round his drab office. He was aware and could see that, from a financial point of view, Tony hadn't been doing well recently. Before he had visited him, he had done his homework. He knew that Tony had become a widower a few years before. He knew that he had a little daughter to care for. He knew that he didn't own his house. He knew that he'd been selling his antiques for a pittance. He had also been told that Tony was always serious, humourless and grey, his best friend a bottle of ouzo.

'You're not young any more,' the marriage-broker snapped after parting with his trench coat. He had rested it carefully next to him on the worn-out sofa where Tony had told him to sit. Each of them had lit a cigarette. They both knew that their discussion wouldn't be concluded in a few minutes. These arrangements would take time. Tony had double-locked the door of the office, out of fear that they might be interrupted and that their secret meeting might be discovered.

'Of course—I know that,' Tony said, irritated.

'And you have a child,' the marriage-broker added.

His technique was to list as many difficulties as possible at the outset, so that his fees could be justified.

'I have to find a wife—but with one condition,' said Tony. 'I don't want to have any children with her.' He got all this out very quickly, in the slight hope that, perhaps by magic, he would be let off the hook.

Mr Theofillos looked at him bluntly and thought to himself: 'I should hope not, you miserable sod.' Then, out loud, he said: 'I understand, but this makes things doubly difficult, you know. All women want to have children. It will be a huge sacrifice on the other party's behalf.'

Quickly Tony rejoined: 'I can provide a good home. I have a good profession. My reputation is…'

'Yes, I know all that. But you're also broke,' the marriage-broker interrupted, implacably.

Tony felt humiliated and angry. Tears throbbed behind his eyes. He gulped to make them disappear. He wanted to grab this man and kick him out. But everything had already gone too far.

'I need a woman with a dowry. Your commission will be good– you know that.'

The broker looked at him thoughtfully as if considering some mental notepad. He was a man of few words; he always tried to be short and to the point. He suddenly remembered a village woman whom he'd tried to marry off many times, but without success. Could he try her out on Tony?

'There's a wonderful rich country spinster available. She has two apartments in town. Her bank account's very healthy. She can cook, embroider and clean. She's healthy and strong. What do you think?'

'Are you positive that she has money?'

'That's been verified by the bank manager, I can assure you.'

Tony didn't want to go any further with the conversation. He quickly accepted the proposal and asked Mr Theofillos to proceed with the necessary arrangements. He was so glad when he had closed the door behind him and his Burberry coat.

Now he knew what to do. He would wait until his proposal was accepted and then he would take the plunge and tell Louisa the truth, coated with the icing sugar of marriage preparations.

Blossom was not thrilled when one lunchtime a professional marriage-broker knocked on their door. He was someone to whom her beloved George had clearly turned as a last resort, under Elektra's guidance.

George had been pushing Blossom to accept this new offer. He had forgotten that she had also accepted all the others, but that the prospective grooms had backed out after they had met her. He had presented Mr Theofillos with a photo for his file, in which Blossom was posing under the Chinese date tree, her face shadowed by its foliage. This same photo had temporarily fooled other prospective suitors.

Her sister-in-law had been even more persistent. As far as Elektra was concerned Blossom had to go, and marriage was the way forward. With bitter sarcasm that Blossom was too dim to understand, Elektra had endlessly praised married life to her. She kept emphasising and repeating that she wanted to see Blossom as happy as she was in her own marriage.

Elektra loathed the closeness between brother and sister, devotion she saw as bordering on the obsessive. Elektra didn't suspect anything perverted; both she and Blossom had been brought up as simple creatures. Once or twice Blossom had dreamt of a most passionate encounter with somebody who had the same kind of aura as her brother, but not his face. She was so innocent that she could never recognise the sinful chemistry between herself and George. She was almost saintly in that respect.

Not long after his arrival, Mr Theofillos was invited to join them for lunch. He refused, apologising for taking their time during a family meal. He never mixed food and business, since it gave him the most dreadful indigestion. He hated sitting at the table to eat, preferring to put his food on a tray and eat on his own while listening to his little radio, carefully following the news. He was embarrassed to eat with others, since his cheap dentures tended to make unpleasant noises, revealing the fact that he was toothless.

He also favoured short meetings, so he wouldn't waste time. Blossom said almost nothing for the whole time he was at George's house, merely nodding her head at the marriage-broker's patter. Mr Theophillos had hoped from the outset that she would be in her usual willing mood and wouldn't dither, so he could soon leave.

He told her: 'There's this gentleman who lives in the best area of the city.' (Kerkyra could hardly be called a city, but Mr Theofillos invariably used the word when he addressed peasant folk.) 'He's looking for a good wife, and I think you're perfect for him.' Her physical ugliness, by now familiar, didn't deter him from pressing on with his task. He asked for permission to light a cigarette, to gain time to mobilise his resources for lying.

He summoned his strength and continued: 'He's a barrister, extremely erudite.' Blossom had no idea what erudite meant. 'He's of the correct age. His apartment's very elegant and well-stocked. He's well-preserved.'

He did not tell her that Tony had sold off most of his beautiful antiques, that he was a heavy smoker, and that he suffered from excruciating migraines, depression and a touch of alcoholism.

'He's always well-dressed,' he continued. 'He hasn't lost any of his dark brown hair and he wears glasses. He's respected in the city, and between us he is quite high up the Masonic ladder.' The last bit of information he imparted while bending his head forward and using a quiet, confidential tone.

George understood immediately, but Blossom thought vaguely that the Masonic ladder must be some kind of scaffolding used to repair her prospective husband's apartment.

'He's a deeply ethical man.' Blossom was lost again at this word. 'He's well-connected. He reads a lot and…' At this point, the broker slowed down. He realised he had exhausted Tony's assets. Now he turned to Blossom, continuing with confidence:

'You'll be the best possible companion for him.' He avoided the word *wife*–after all, he had no idea what Blossom's qualities in that area could possibly be, apart from her big, full purse.

'He appreciates good food, and you must be excellent at providing that.'

Blossom smiled at this flattery and nodded in agreement.

'He was married before,' he added in haste, 'but his wife died three years ago, leaving him with a little six-year-old girl. She is nine now. I strongly believe that both of them will be an excellent addition to your wonderful family.'

Blossom looked at her brother, who had remained silent throughout the presentation. 'This is a gift–a child for all of us. I shall take care of her and love her so that we won't be a barren family any more,' Blossom thought.

She had made up her mind. She couldn't think of a single reservation. Everything this man said about her prospective husband was too good to be true. She had kept silent out of courtesy. Now, out loud, she asked: 'What's her name?'–referring to Louisa.

'I have no idea,' replied Mr Theofillos, slightly embarrassed. He had never thought of asking for any details about the little girl. Although the whole transaction would be of great benefit to Tony's daughter, the child was surely irrelevant in terms of the current negotiations.

'That's a strange question, but a hopeful response,' he thought. 'It indicates acceptance rather than curiosity.'

'Do you accept the offer?' he asked, with a silent sigh of relief.

George nodded in agreement. 'Excellent,' the marriage-broker said cheerfully. He stamped his cigarette butt on the heavy metal ashtray which was a replica of an aeroplane landing on a dish airport, and got up. 'I must go and give the good news,' he declared.

He grabbed his trench coat from the seat next to him. He was so anxious to conclude the deal that he almost forgot to say a cordial good-bye. George grabbed him by the arm and thanked him profusely, with an additional 'God bless you' and 'We hope we'll see you very soon.'

Mr Theofillos went straight to Tony to give him the glad tidings.

It was Louisa's third year of primary school, and as always, on the way there she would try hard to refrain from staring at the other children holding their mothers by the hand. Mothers were everywhere she looked. They turned up at break time to supplement the basic cheese-pie with fruit, juice and sweets. They turned up to collect their children at the end of lessons, to accompany them home. They turned up to help the teachers decorate the classrooms. They talked among themselves about everybody and everything.

Louisa would walk sadly to school by herself. She would eat her pre-packed sandwiches, suffering enormously from the glances of pity and sadness directed towards her by the other children's mothers. She would offer a little money towards the classroom decorations, instead of parental participation. She was fully aware that everyone knew everything about her predicament. They pitied her loneliness. She felt deeply embarrassed, annoyed and powerless.

It was only when the school bell rang to summon the pupils back into their classrooms that she felt a stab of joy. Now she was like everyone else. At the end of the school day, mothers would again gather to collect their children and walk them home. Louisa would be the only one trailing along behind, not holding a mother's protective hand. *Oh well...* she thought. She would jump, laugh, joke and sing silly songs on her own. Never mind how much she wished she could vanish each afternoon from the face of the earth.

There were other things she hated apart from going to school motherless. She hated the fact that her nanny had been dismissed. She had loved Tina second only to her mother, and missed her terribly. The home she and Tony shared was empty, gloomy and serious. Her father, without the support of women, had to do their work. Louisa's clothes were not as well-pressed as before, the organdie dresses with matching hats vanished, and her hair was cut short so that nobody was needed to care for it daily.

Most of all she loathed the food they ate. Gone were the elaborate menus, the lovely syrupy cakes. Since her mother and the maid had left, *cannelloni*, much-adored *schnitzel* and *lasagne* had all vanished from their family menu, replaced by dreaded bean soup, lentils, chick peas and (horror of horrors) dried salted cod, soaked overnight and then cooked in tomato sauce with potatoes. Every time Louisa put it in her mouth, she felt she was eating a mouthful of cotton wool.

As she grew older, she was developing an extremely sensitive stomach. The family doctor had explained that the tempestuous boat journey to and from Athens might have caused this. Louisa herself reckoned it was the wretched menu she had to eat every day. Casual vomiting had become a habit with her that would unfortunately plague her for the rest of her life.

One lunchtime in mid-September, after the first couple of days of the school term, she returned from school dreading the prospect of cod. It was Friday, the unavoidable day for fish. She climbed the stairs, avoiding the cats' faeces inexpertly covered with sand, and entered the apartment. It already stank of cod.

Her father was standing by the window in the dining room. Without greeting her, he cleared his throat with a rough cough. Then he said: 'Louisa, sit down…' She could tell that he wanted to tell her something important, but was having difficulty spelling it out.

'You're going to have a new mother,' he said plainly and coldly. 'Your own mother has been dead now for three years. I'm going to get married to another woman. You can call her 'Mother' or 'Mum' or 'Mummy'. The wedding is on Sunday. This is for you, for your own good.'

He said the whole thing all in one breath. Then he rattled on: 'Your mother has been dead now for three years. She died in hospital just a few days before our return here. I didn't tell you. I thought you were too young to understand. Now the time has come for you to have another mother, a new mother.'

Louisa received this news without a trace of surprise. Within a fraction of a second she was transformed into a middle-aged woman, hardened and empty of emotion. She had sensed the truth for some time now, but had never wanted to bring the subject into the open. At the same time she had clung to the idea that she might wake one morning to find everything changed by magic, back to what had been before.

Now she realised that miracles never happen.

She looked at Tony, who kept staring out the window at the passers-by. She fumbled with the hem of her school uniform with her thin little fingers.

'I knew my mother was dead,' she said. 'You kept it a secret from me—but I knew all the time. You told me she stayed behind in the hospital to get better. But I knew you were telling lies.'

'You're going to have a new dress and new shoes for the wedding. You're going to be a bridesmaid,' blundered Tony.

Louisa shed no tears; she was not upset, just numb. She felt neither pain nor sadness. Like a calculating adult and with extraordinary speed she came to perceive the forthcoming marriage as an adventure, something that would add spice to their dull life. She turned her back on her father and left the room, jumping and hopping.

Blossom and Tony's wedding was not a happy event. Only Blossom was mildly content with the way things had turned out. She had quite liked Tony the first time she met him. The day of the wedding was the second time they met, and she continued to like him. He was quiet and solemn, but she didn't care. When asked, years later, what she liked best about him, she replied: 'I looked at his well-polished shoes, and I loved the way the laces were done up. I also fell in love with Louisa. I wanted to look after her and love her to the end of my days.'

In the church where the ceremony took place there were no flowers or decorations. Everyone involved was middle-aged and tired. They all wanted the event over and done with. Tony said 'yes' full of regret and remorse. Until the day of his death he never forgave himself for committing such an act of hypocrisy. He had disliked Blossom from the very first.

Never was a couple more unsuited than these two. When the priest passed the chalice with the wine, Tony nearly spat it out in disgust. It tasted like vinegar in his dry mouth, in spite of the fact that George had boasted it was from the best stock in his cellar. Blossom drank it without wincing. She thought it the sweetest thing she'd ever tasted.

Louisa kept fumbling with her hem. She started to teach herself mentally to say the word 'Mummy'. She focused on Blossom's appearance and her wiry hair. But her eyes were flooded with tears.

A big lunch followed. Tony hardly touched his food. Blossom devoured the lot. Louisa ran out to the olive grove and vomited under a huge tree.

The following Monday morning Louisa arrived at school accompanied by her new 'mother'. There were three long years between Poppy leaving on a stretcher and Blossom moving into Louisa's house, planning to become its mistress.

Immediately after the wedding, alone with Blossom for the first time, Tony realised the huge mistake he'd made. Blossom was now his wife. He couldn't ignore her the way he ignored others, like maids and nannies, and yet he began to do so, without remorse. He continually lost his temper at her stupidity, her funny peasant ways. He became deeply embarrassed by her presence. She was a kind woman, but her uncouth ways were too much for him. He was deeply ashamed of what he'd done.

To cope, he became even more solemn and uncommunicative. He carried on drinking his small tumblers of ouzo accompanied by the little round white aspirin, a couple at a time. The lime trees in the square gave him shade, but no comfort. His remoteness made life with him impossible. He read his books and never spoke except to give orders to Blossom. He treated her as if everything that went wrong was her fault.

Blossom cleaned up after the cats, cooked the most delicious meals, did the washing and ironing and made the beds. The apartment was Louisa's entire world, the space where her mother had existed. She loved whatever was left of her, the paintings and furniture more than anything. Her toys and one doll in particular made up her private world.

Tony, Blossom and Louisa hardly ever went out together. Louisa became paler, Blossom fatter and Tony kept on smelling faintly of ouzo and tobacco.

And what of Elektra and George? Up until their deaths, in spite of their peculiarities and inability to bring children into the world, in the eyes of the villagers George and Elektra were the perfect, respectable, well-to-do couple: straight, formal, unsmiling and of real substance in the community. George's passion continued to be non-existent and Elektra continued to focus on her chickens.

Chapter 3

Portovecchio's sea air fills with the heavenly smell of *frigathelia*, while the priest prepares *savouro*

I have a problem with Temptation,
As well as Transubstantiation.

I marvel at the Maker,
The Dimiourgos,
The Poet, the Plastis.

I praise all the glories of Creation.
But I have a problem
With Temptation.

Summer 1956

Portovecchio is a seaside suburb of Kerkyra. Its main road didn't always follow the coast, as it does now. It used to run through Portovecchio's heart, with houses and shops on either side. The buildings which stood between the road and the sea had a beach full of seaweed at the end of their back gardens. Most of its people were fishermen, slaughterhouse labourers or had jobs in the shipyard. Others worked eight-hour shifts in the flour mill or the olive oil processing factory. The women knitted fishing nets, worked as maids in the capital, and were the best dressmakers on the island. Many of them, whether married or not, were the mistresses of some gentleman in town.

Portovecchio was insignificant in the larger scheme of Hellenic history. Only occasionally had it featured in any event of importance. In 1799 it had participated in a revolt against the French, but socially and historically speaking, its great contribution to the island was the plentiful supply of fresh fish. It also provided smuggled cigarettes and an endless supply of good-looking mistresses. For all these resources the inhabitants of Kerkyra were grateful to the inhabitants of Portovecchio, and mindful of paying them generously and promptly.

Fat Foni didn't have to go to town to meet her lover. She was mistress-supreme to the parish priest, Father Anthony. Knitting fishing nets was not one of her strengths. Her husband, old Paul, had retired from fishing at a very early age, due to two unfortunate circumstances. First, as a youth, he had lost his left arm while practising his favourite fishing method: using dynamite to kill the fish. Then osteoporosis afflicted him to such an extent that he was now bent almost double. He moved along painfully with his upper torso parallel to the ground and at right angles to his legs, his face and eyes forced to stare straight down at the ground. When he slept, he had to lie on his side. Sex between him and Foni had been non-existent since time immemorial. So she was thrilled at the opportunity to take Father Anthony as an eager lover. He supplied her with everything she desired, without her needing to commute. The priest was very local indeed.

This passionate lover was also welcomed as a guest by Paul.

During summer evenings at around six and after their siesta, young and old gathered outside their front doors on the main road. They turned their backs to the sea. These evening gatherings gave them a break from the ever-present sea, with its associations of labour and hardship.

Portovecchio at this time had no fancy fish restaurants. Fish was plentiful and cheap, caught daily by one-third of its population. Nobody had to go to a restaurant to eat it. The Portovecchio inhabitants' idea of eating out was to indulge in a certain type of take-away bought from dingy little taverns scattered throughout the suburb. The cost was negligible even by their standards. The take-away consisted of a tiny kebab called *frigatheli*, a little piece of calf's liver and then two pieces of juicy fat alternated on a short, sharpened bamboo skewer. The *frigatheli* had been drenched in oregano, salt, pepper and lemon and grilled on an open charcoal fire. It was invariably accompanied by brown bread, which was called black bread. The bread stood at the point of the skewer, and when it was handed over by the tavern keeper it resembled an ugly open umbrella. Everybody's mouth watered at the thought of *frigathelia*.

Portovecchio evenings were enveloped in a haze of highly-scented charcoal smoke as the grilling started, around sunset. Nowadays there are plenty of up-market fish restaurants frequented by locals and foreigners alike. Their fish dishes are priced astronomically high, since the fish is imported from as far away as the Bosphorus. Dynamiting has taken its toll on the fish of Portovecchio. Today's fashionable restaurants have views of the substantial harbour, extended half a mile beyond the old shoreline. The sea has been reclaimed and the water in the harbour is now very deep, accommodating luxury cruisers, large ferries and expensive yachts. In those days the vessels moored at the rickety wooden jetties used to be working fishing boats. Sometimes, when not out on business, they were used for family swimming outings. Arrivals and departures of ferryboats and big cruise ships were not an hourly event then as they are now.

These days, the new national road takes all the traffic away from the heart of Portovecchio. This is good for the place, since the traffic has increased a thousand-fold. It bypasses the old central road, leaving it relatively free from air pollution and noise. But no-one can see who is coming and going. Private cars reach the main road as soon as they set off.

Portovecchio's air was always laden with smells. If they didn't come from the *frigatheli*, they were mixed with the reek of the boiling tar used at the small shipyards. These two odours, with those from the olive oil processing factory and the slaughterhouse, which was in action three times a week, made Portovecchio the most strangely perfumed place in the universe.

Nobody minded; they all knew where each smell came from. There were clear days, of course, and the abundance of jasmine, honeysuckle, roses, lemon and orange blossom, which grew away from the piles of seaweed, created a fusion of aromas that made Portovecchio an earthly paradise by the sea. There was one smell in particular that incited the imagination of the inhabitants, and made them extra amorous. It was the sweet smell of sage that rose in August after a heavy storm. New liaisons blossomed at that time of the year. Was it the heavenly smell of sage that inspired Father Anthony to turn to

Fat Foni? Some said yes; others who knew him better declared: 'He's just a horny, nasty piece of work.'

In the winter no-one took a siesta, because just after midday, the sun was at its warmest. Everyone used this natural source of heat and took up their positions on the front porch, after the lunchtime washing-up, to keep warm. They baked themselves in the sun to store enough heat in their bones for the long, freezing winter nights.

The women gossiped, worked on their nets with a speed that made one dizzy just looking at them, or dressed up and took the bus into town. The ones left behind knew that most of the female bus passengers were going to meet the unfaithful husbands of other women. These mistresses were extravagantly decorated. Their boyfriends were always generous to them, out of fear they might be abandoned, or the mistresses become indiscreet out of spite. They dressed up in the latest garish fashions, with high heels as essential accessories. Peroxide blonde was their favourite hair colour. These women were affluent; they were among the very few in Pontovecchio who didn't need other employment.

Again, Fat Foni was the exception. Her hair was dyed jet black and she had to work in the mill. Her husband's pension was small, and the priest's family enormous. After every visit to her house for 'a cup of coffee' (as he used to say), he would surreptitiously leave under a saucer just enough money for Paul's evening backgammon game. Paul played with his right hand while his left shirt sleeve hung empty, the end tucked inside his shiny black polyester trousers.

Neighbours would raise their eyebrows when the priest emerged from Fat Foni's door. He would depart with a gruff *au revoir*, while she crossed herself three times behind his back. She didn't really like his black cassock; she associated it with death.

Father Anthony normally only visited the homes of his parishioners when somebody was dying. If he was seen emerging from a cottage, his cassock belted tight around his waist, everybody knew that somebody inside was ready to depart for the other world. But every Portovecchian knew that death wasn't responsible for Father Anthony's visits to Fat Foni's home. Elaborate, fancy and passionate sex took place three times a week in the little whitewashed cottage with the green shutters and the vine creeping around its door. Everybody bet that Paul, because of his osteoporosis, was incapable of seeing anything that went on around him. Even if he did, they surmised, he must turn a blind eye.

The Portovecchio men were of average height and were extremely light in build. Their faces were craggy, their noses crooked. The absence of any substantial fat was not due to lack of food; on the contrary, their diet of mostly fish and fruit made them exceptionally healthy. It was the hard work that used up the fat and left them skin and bone. Their faces were darkly tanned and wrinkled so that they resembled dried prunes on sticks. This added nothing to their sex appeal. If the women were garrulous, the men were mostly silent and remote, shy and thoughtful, constantly smoking cigarettes and enjoying a drink or two in the evenings.

The priest was different. He was tall, with short thick curly red hair and a well-trimmed beard of an orange hue. He was well-built and had extravagant hazel eyes. He never went to join the other men for a drink or to sit with them by the roadside. He preferred Fat Foni's cottage. There, when not fornicating, he held court with a group of women, mostly widows, elaborating on the theme of God. He would drink his coffee sitting comfortably on Fat Foni's hard sofa, beneath the portraits of the King and Queen of the Hellenes, Jesus Christ looking up at a sparkling blue sky, and a solemn portrait of Fat Foni's parents. Whenever he was found alone there with Fat Foni, she would treat him with generosity to a couple of small glasses of her sweet and sticky cumquat.

Father Anthony was confident he could have found another, far more beautiful woman willing to serve him, such a worthy man of God was he. Fat Foni was not exactly Miss Portovecchio. But he had decided not to go with other women. In his heart, he recognised his inability to offer them what others could give them. So it was either Fat Foni or–if he were to be one hundred per cent honest, which was not his habit–another lady with whom he was sincerely, passionately and obsessively in love.

Unfortunately, up till now, she had not been destined for him. Who knew about the future? Perhaps sometime soon? She was the most beautiful lady in Portovecchio–or even further afield. Her name was Zoë and she had a little daughter called Maria. She had been a widow for some years. The Hellenic state, and of course His Eminence, were responsible for that. Ever since her husband's execution, she had been living with her mother-in-law, her daughter and a heart-wrenching letter in a drawer.

The priest, in his priestly robe and in the name of God, tried to give her psychological support. Although before his death they had known each other for a long time, Father Anthony and her husband John found differences regarding the philosophy and theory of life had created a gulf between them in their adult lives. When John had been taken from her, the priest had stood by the widow like a good Christian. Portovecchio had judged this as the act of a holy man. Nobody knew that he'd loved Zoë all his life, and very few suspected his testimony to the police department, which in fact had led to John's arrest.

As well as with Zoë; Father Anthony had also, since he was very young, been obsessed with Hellenic Christian ideology. God and Country were tightly connected in his brain. Not having much money to fund his purpose in life, he paved his way by marrying money. He found a bride who came with a handsome, substantially-sized house that would serve as a vicarage and was also one of the loveliest residences in Portovecchio. In Father Anthony's thinking, the Almighty required elaborate real estate. He secretly admired the Vatican, although he often attacked it in his sermons. He was a devout man of contradictions. He believed that God and grandeur, dressing up and cheating often went together.

Father Anthony's wife, young, plain and stupid at the time of their marriage, had become a washed-out blonde with ice-cold blue eyes. After numerous pregnancies and many babies, she had devised a cocktail of tranquillisers that destroyed her appetite for sex forever. Her husband, highly-sexed, turned to Fat Foni.

His wife had decided to provoke him. She had adopted the habit of walking round the house with her breasts hanging out 'in order to save time undressing', she declared, when she had to feed one of their babies. This was one reason Father Anthony ran across the road to Fat Foni. She was for him a wife replacement from within the Christian community, the neighbourhood and the church committee. Her caresses reassured him that he was still a living man. Fat Foni would fervently offer this reassurance. There was absolutely nothing wrong with him, she would say during foreplay. She kept putting aside the notion that there was another woman occupying his real affections. As for Father Anthony, he imagined another on top of him as he lay almost buried underneath Fat Foni's ample body. He was fantasising about Zoë.

Fat Foni had many advantages. She could never have children; a couple of abortions at an early age had left her barren. She cost very little, since she agreed to sleep with him for the prestige of being close to the church rather than for material profit. Through sex she had become the power behind all parish affairs. The priest's lust was moderately satisfied; he was only doing what he could afford, after all. His family budget was well-balanced and always within its limits. Nor was his wife bothered by his continuous needs.

The houses of Portovecchio, apart from God's residence and a few other exceptions, consisted of small, simple cottages. The alleys off the main road were narrow, whitewashed and spotlessly clean. Apart from being fishy and inhabited by generous mistresses, Portovecchio's reputation throughout the island was for feisty women who shouted and screamed at the slightest provocation, and for men who, although aggressive when provoked, calmly turned a blind eye to the escapades of their wives. The wives' comings and goings invariably helped alleviate their economic burdens, so the husbands weren't too bothered. Brothers and fathers would occasionally get upset, especially when a bastard was produced and they became responsible for its upkeep. Fights would then break out. Chairs with seats of woven straw, as featured in most Hellenic Tourist Organisation promotional posters, were the chosen weapons. These chairs, objects of 'beautiful Hellenic design', had three uses: first as weapons of anger; second to provide rest for weary feet; and third to promote the country abroad. They were not very good for any of them.

Although most housing was cramped, with three generations often living in one room, cleanliness was next to Godliness. The rooms in which people lived and slept were spotless. The houses were turned inside out every day. The bedding was aired daily and the carpets beaten and shaken in the wind after the bedding had been taken in. Lime was used in abundance to paint walls, the trunks of trees and pots. The houses shone brilliantly in the sunshine, washed from top to bottom by the plentiful Portovecchian rain.

Monday was washing day. On Sunday night all white clothes were put to soak in a different bucket from the dark-coloured washing, with plenty of laurel leaves and olive oil-based soap dissolved in the water. On Monday mornings, all the washing was vigorously scrubbed on washboards, a back-breaking task. Strangely enough, no-one ever complained. The washing was dried on a long line in front of each house, supported by a broom-stick in the middle. It was never hung from house to house, as along the alleys in the capital. Portovecchio houses were mostly single-storey.

The wind blew the washing in all directions, flapping the bed sheets with gusto. In spite of this, the washing took a long time to dry, since the climate was so humid. On Mondays, the children played hide-and-seek all round the white washing with its slight tint of blue rinse. Sometimes they buried their faces in the drying sheets with childish giggles, to inhale the delicious laurel-leaf perfume.

Inside the houses in those days, there was no washing machine, no tumble dryer, no television, no telephone, no fridge. There was no laundry and no bathroom. Face washing was done over the kitchen sink. Very often there was no lavatory. If a house enjoyed the luxury of a toilet, it was always placed in a tiny cubicle within the kitchen. The previous days' newspapers were cut into neat squares and hung from some wire next to the lavatory seat to serve as the best paper in the world.

Families who didn't have an inside lavatory owned a grand chamber pot with a lid. Everyone used it, and the mother of the house had to empty it into the sea at the end of the seaweed-filled garden every morning before sunrise.

The gardens bloomed with all the flowers the Mediterranean basin can sustain. White lilies, geraniums, bougainvillea, freesias, irises, gardenias, hydrangeas, oleander, honeysuckle, jasmine and basil were found on every corner. The trees produced tasty fruit: plums galore, lemons and oranges, almonds, figs, prickly pears and apricots. There was no possibility of anyone going hungry. All stomachs were full, even if pockets were two-thirds empty.

The proximity of the sea was what made Portovecchio special. The smells, the buzz of daily activity, the lime whitewash, the fruit, the women's shouting and chatter, all derived from its position and made it unique. The men walked around with bare feet, their trousers rolled up to their knees. They carried baskets full of fish and the nets they used to catch them.

Father Anthony was not allowed to carry anything except the chalice to administer the last rites. If somebody was dying he would be called out, and with his robes flapping, holding the silver Holy Cup containing the flesh and blood of Christ in his hands, he would swirl mystically around the suburb. The purple robe that protruded from under his black cassock added to his outlandish appearance.

His reputation with the dying was excellent. He specialised in aiding the departing. Unfortunately, he was motivated by little other than self-gratification. His skill was not enough to satisfy his real god, the greed that lived within him and could never be named or identified. He found roundabout ways to supplement his income, and to glorify his God.

The preparation of students for their religious exams was one way; the other had been his appointment at the local prison a few years earlier as *priest extraordinaire*. At the height of the Civil War he had applied for and secured the position of confessor and witness at the prison. This was where all the Communists were locked up and kept until their transportation to the island of Lazaretto, where they were executed. His job was to be at their side to the last: hearing their last confession–rarely given–and giving them their last Communion. Then he would witness their execution. They were always executed facing the wall, not the firing squad. When they were shot, their bodies collapsed like marionettes whose strings had suddenly been cut.

Father Anthony would stand and stare at their ragged clothes against the green and blue landscape of the little island. His presence infuriated the prisoners, since none of them believed in the church, 'the opium of the people'. To him they were monsters of evil condemned to Hell, whose existence he never questioned. He occasionally experienced uneasy stirrings of doubt, but believed that, as God's agent on this earth, he was safe from the fires. Sometimes when he was mechanically chanting during the Sunday service, he wondered whether any priest in the world really believed absolutely that God and the Devil existed. He wondered if he would ever find the answer.

Some of his colleagues admired his bravery in accepting the job at the prison. No other priest on the island was willing to carry out such a task. Eventually, with the ending of the Civil War, the post was abolished, and Father Anthony's income was again reduced. Not only did he miss the extra cash, but also the frisson of seeing the Communists collapse at the wall.

He well remembered John, pacing angrily in his tiny cell, demanding and begging him to leave Zoë alone. He had tried to wipe John from his mind, John with his wild, tremulous glance, whispering: 'You'll never have Zoë.' Perhaps, thought Father Anthony, he had never actually heard this. Since John's death, he had never stopped being extra-friendly and caring towards her. Deep in his black heart he hoped that one day Fat Foni, his wife and the Bishop who controlled his life would all drop dead, to be replaced by Zoë.

The Civil War had been over for some years now. Most of the 'Red parasites' were dead and buried. The church continued to run like clockwork. Fat Foni carried on serving cumquat to the priest. The dying took Father Anthony's image with them to Eternity. The priest's wife still wandered around the house barely dressed, and her husband dreamed about Zoë.

One day his neighbours noticed that a black-and-white cat had started following Father Anthony around everywhere he went, even into the rooms of the dying, Fat Foni or gentle Zoë.

'Fuck you, get away!' he would shout at the cat, through clenched teeth. When he reckoned nobody was looking he would give the poor animal a vicious kick. His new escort was driving him to distraction. Sometimes the cat would turn and run away, but at other times she would pursue the priest right up to the deathbed he was visiting, despite his cursing and shooing.

This attachment had no supernatural cause; the cat's attraction to the priest was purely culinary. Father Anthony was the best cook of *savouro* in Portovecchio.

The recipe had come to him directly from his mother, born and bred in the suburb she never left. The fishermen of Portovecchio, always wanting to be in God's good books, were extremely generous to Father Anthony. He was to them the go-between to God, in all times of need but especially during the autumnal storms, when the sea became so wild. Throughout the year they would provide him and his family with unlimited fish–which of course cost them nothing. Father Anthony never refused these gifts, and he took great delight in cooking them. His wife never helped. She was sick of cooking for, breeding and living with him. She couldn't do anything to change the last, although managed to put a stop to the first two.

Every day after his morning church service, Father Anthony would enter the kitchen and start by cleaning, but never washing the day's fish. 'There's no point,' he'd insist. 'It came from the water, didn't it?' He always separated out the big fish for grilling, frying and stewing, using the smaller ones to make the best *savouro* in the world. Once he'd collected all the little ones he'd dip them in seasoned flour. He would put plenty of olive oil in a huge frying pan–and he was never economical about the oil, because this was also a gift from the parishioners to the church. They saw it as their duty to provide plenty of olive oil for its lamps. Their offering was enough to light the whole *ecoumeni*, so a cup here and there was never missed.

After the fish was fried, he'd take it out of the pan and put it in layers in a clay pot. The concept of measurement in cooking was too subtle for the priest. He mixed things according to his taste. He followed this rule even with Holy Communion: plenty of sugar, red wine and enough water to make an average-sized bottle go round the entire congregation, the faithful and the unfaithful. He followed the same principle with his cooking: everything according to his personal preference. He would make the rennete by mixing more flour in the hot pan and stirring it at a low heat until it browned. Then he would add all the rest of the ingredients: plenty of sea salt, pepper, vinegar, white wine, sultanas, whole cloves of garlic and plenty of tomato paste diluted with water. Just as he did every Sunday with the Holy Communion, he would pour plenty of sugar into his *savouro*, because this is how he liked them both: sweet and sharp. The herbs he used were limited to laurel leaves and rosemary. He loved rosemary, and always used the whole bunch that had previously, during the service, sprinkled Holy Water over his congregation. Rosemary was plentiful around the church, and in every corner of the garden there was a rosemary bush growing out of a whitewashed pot. Fat Foni and the priest's wife looked after them, in turn.

The smell of rosemary reminded him of the holy atmosphere of the church. It certainly helped him to make his *savouro*. After he'd boiled the rennete in the frying pan for a couple of minutes, he would pour it into the clay pot, then put the lid on and leave it like this for a couple of days, until the flavours had blended. Then the *savouro* was ready to eat. The beauty of this dish was that it could last for a week in the hot climate without having to be put in the icebox. The vinegar and wine took care of that.

When the cooking of the fish was finished, he threw the entrails to the cat. This is why she began to follow Father Anthony everywhere he went.

The daily routine of Portovecchio was determined by its seasons. In the autumn, there were the storms, the rain, the name days, and leaving off swimming in the sea. In the winter there were brilliant, cold sunny days that dried the washing in a flash. In the summer there was the swimming, the fishing and the daily passing of the Royal Family. This provided a regular spectacle for everyone, especially the young. Every day at four in the afternoon, three jeeps with their cloth hoods down, loaded up with the Hellenic Royal Family would pass through the neighbourhood. The King would be in the driver's seat of the first jeep; the Queen would be next to him, and their two daughters would be sitting in the back. In the second jeep the heir to the throne would be in charge, accompanied by a few friends. In the third vehicle would ride a couple of the most handsome soldier-guards that Greece had available that particular year.

At four o'clock only the children were not taking their siesta. Almost all the adults were lying on their beds, exhausted by the heat and trying to find relief in their airless rooms. The children would shout all together: 'The King, the King!' and clap their hands. The Royal party would give them the Royal wave, then drive off to the country.

The Portovecchio children wondered where they went each day. All this stopped when the Royal family was sent into exile, their summer holidays in Kerkyra a pleasure of the past. 'Good riddance!' reckoned many adult inhabitants of Portovecchio. Father Anthony was the only one who felt really angry. He was silently enraged at the loss of Christian Hellas' monarchy.

The people of Portovecchio rarely turned to the metropolis for their services. This was not only because their suburb offered anything they wanted, but also because they needed so little. At six every morning, daylight in summer but pitch black in winter, the factory labourers ventured out, still half-asleep, summoned by the piercing sirens of the factory and the mill. They would go off to earn their living while the women began their housework, at the same time inquisitively scrutinising everything that was going on in Portovecchio around them. In their free time, with its swimming, gossip, cafés, church and fiestas, it became their playground. It was rarely visited by the town folk, so its beauty was not experienced–except by hear-say–by those from the outside world.

Where Portovecchio was obscure, Kerkyra was famous. But Kerkyra has faded now. There is no Odysseus hovering around his Nausicaa; there are no rich Venetians taking a break from the Serene Republic; there are not even any British intellectuals of the kind who helped make the island so famous.

Portovecchio has weathered better. It still has a certain fishy charm. Modern morality has abolished the institution of the mistress, and the little skewered morsels of pork have become oversized kebabs. The priest and his wife are long since dead and gone, and the nuns have installed Fat Foni and her husband in the old people's home they run.

But Father Anthony's substantial home still stands next to the grand house of God and still looks the same, if a little neglected. Across it there is an enormous skeleton of cement where a block of apartments will be built. This space, at the time of our story, contained the white house with its geraniums, its enormous fruit trees, its water pump and its bougainvillea, which was to receive Tony, Blossom and Louisa less than a year after the autumnal wedding.

Chapter 4

A new home, the slaughterhouse, pea stew and *kerkiraiko bourdeto*

Young girls stare at fishermen with nets:
The cats are all eyes
For the fish.

Summer 1956

In July and August, humidity affects everything on Kerkyra. The washing never dries, scalps itch, hair curls up tightly, arthritis flares, nerves are frayed and mist shrouds the island. Everyone hopes that by midday the dampness will lift and that they'll survive another day.

One morning in mid-July it was especially hot and humid in Portovecchio. The sun was emerging slowly, intent on dazzling and scorching the earth and its inhabitants. It hadn't as yet had time to uncurl Father Anthony's red hair and beard and calm his nerves. He came out of the church at full speed and quickly headed for Fat Foni's cottage. There he hoped he'd find some comfort.

He glanced round quickly to make sure that nobody was looking, then rushed across the road. The handsome black-

and-white cat kept pace behind him like a child following its father. As soon as the priest entered the little gate into the garden, he turned round to send her away with some very un-Christian language, She ran, jumped and curled up on the gatepost, next to a clay pot of bright red geraniums with velvety green foliage.

The cat was wearing a red neck-collar with a small tin bell hanging from it. A ten-year-old girl, who was standing a little further away, approached her with gestures of affection. She stretched out her arm to stroke her, but the cat uncurled swiftly, jumped to one side and ran away under the bougainvillea hedge to the neighbour's garden. The little girl was startled. She had stepped back in fright, thinking the cat was going to attack, jump at her face and scratch her. She had once seen a film in which lions and bears viciously attacked their victims. They had devoured them: only bones, skin and blood were left.

The little girl screamed and ran indoors into the kitchen, where a short, round woman with tightly-curled black hair and bow legs was standing in front of the paraffin stove. She was stirring food in a wide, flat saucepan. She wore a dark green apron over a flowery dress, the kind of apron that peasant women usually wear tied round their waist twice. The apron was covered in grease stains. The wooden spoon in the woman's hand was too large for the height of the saucepan, but she kept stirring. There was an overpowering smell of fried onions. On the kitchen-table was a pile of sliced aubergines, another of parsley, and a third of fresh, bright red chopped tomatoes.

The girl was crying and yelling. She needed comforting. She wanted to run and bury herself in her mother's arms, to be kissed and cuddled. Instinct made her suddenly stop a couple of feet away from the woman. She carried on crying but couldn't let herself run into her arms. Forces stronger than her fear held her back. She simply stood stock-still in the middle of the small kitchen, as if somebody had nailed her to the floor. She didn't want this woman to touch her. She didn't want to be crushed against the dirty apron, with the woman's sweat in her nostrils. This woman wasn't her mother.

'Don't cry–she's a good cat,' the woman said kindly. She had been watching the little girl through the open window. Then suddenly Louisa stopped crying. She gulped, to suppress her emotions, deciding she didn't want to be comforted. She turned and ran into the dining room, grabbed her doll and ran out again. Where could she go? Back to the front garden, as far away from the kitchen as possible.

The heat was unbearable. Louisa was wearing a dark blue sleeveless dress with tiny white dots. It was made of very stiff organdie, and her little lace petticoat showed through, since the organdie was transparent. The dress made her feel sweaty and uncomfortable. It was the kind of thing that wealthy little girls would wear to see *The Nutcracker* at Christmas. Kerkyra offered no such entertainments. The dress had been bought for her from a woman in their old neighbourhood who imported second-hand American clothes and cast-offs. These had been sent overseas for charity, but in fact they were used to make money for a self-appointed agent. Twice a year the woman-agent invited all the neighbours to her house and showed them the delivery. Then all of them picked some garments out, tried them on and, if they liked them and they fitted, bought them.

This was so much cheaper than buying clothes in the shops, and the garments were first class American quality–at least that's what people reckoned. On this particular day, Louisa's dress felt as uncomfortable as a straightjacket. Every so often she wiggled in discomfort.

She went to stand again by the gate, the bougainvillea above her providing a little shade. The temperature was well into the thirties. All the houses had their window shutters closed to keep the heat out. It was the kind of heat that makes you lazy, the kind that makes your eyelids stick together as the drops of sweat trickle down from your forehead. In such weather the people of Portovecchio stayed indoors in darkened spaces, keeping flies, mosquitoes and heat out. All activity in the streets ceased by 10 o'clock. Then they were deserted. Everyone settled down in their workplaces, while the housewives made themselves busy in the cool of their homes.

The girl's face was subdued as she looked at the empty street. She had hardly noticed Father Anthony in his black cassock.

Louisa's house was one of three situated high up on top of the hill called Portovecchio Head. The neighbourhood had been described and represented to her as a place where all her bad memories would disappear and where a new beginning would make her happier. But *Lethe* was not an option for Louisa. Two houses, hers and another, stood next to each other. Immediately opposite was the priest's house. The houses were both divided and joined by small, lush gardens.

A fourth house stood opposite. It looked distinguished and stylish with its classical symmetry. It was pale yellow and there were neat, light curtains at the windows. Louisa thought that this house was even prettier than theirs.

Tony, Blossom and Louisa had moved into their white house the previous day. This was why Louisa didn't know anybody in Portovecchio Head.

This part of the suburb felt itself to be superior to the rest. For Louisa everything was new and very strange. It was the first time she and her family were going to have a garden or live by the sea. She wondered why they had left their city apartment, the place where she'd been born and lived all her short life, in order to stay here away from everything and everybody. So far she had not explored the back garden or enjoyed the view of the sea. After she had familiarised herself with the inside of the house, she stuck to the front gate. The need for human contact and some thread connecting her with the past kept her there. She could look back down the road from where they had come, the path leading back to her old life.

The back door of the house was still blocked with packing cases. Huge trees screened the sea view from the back windows. It was really a lovely house, with all the rooms on ground level and doors and windows opening out into the garden. There were plum, almond, orange and lemon trees and many rose bushes, daisies and honeysuckle. There were bougainvillea creepers and white lilies with huge green leaves. The house was white and its shutters a very dark cypress green. The flowers gave the whole scene a homely touch.

But if the house appeared attractive and cheerful, Louisa's heart was elsewhere. She was sad, terribly sad, and lonely. Her old home had been so close to her school. Where would she go to school this coming September? All her friends had been left behind. The memories of her mother were also part of the old home. She couldn't find her mother in this new house, no matter how hard she tried.

Leaning against the gatepost, she stopped crying. She crossed her arms on her flat chest, embracing her doll as tightly as possible, and stroking her arms. Her flesh was damp because of the humidity, but cool in spite of the heat. Stroking herself gave her comfort. The doll's face touched her sweating cheek. She loved the feel of the porcelain face, but to be touched by anybody else would feel like a violation of her mother's rights, and a betrayal. Nobody else could have a claim on her any more. She only loved her doll.

This doll had an indirect connection with her mother. An aunt of hers from Los Angeles had sent it to console her after her mother was no longer there to care for her any more.

The new woman who was cooking indoors was very different from the mother she remembered. Louisa had been puzzled ever since the day of the wedding. Why do people marry again and again? Why do they marry at all? Why did they now need a third person to join them?

Suddenly the door of the pretty house across the street opened and two girls came out. One was older than Louisa, the other younger. The first was carrying a rag-doll, while the younger was pulling a doll's pram. The girls looked at her from across the street. Their faces were tanned and serious, and their clothes casual, but neat and smart. Very timidly they walked towards her.

'Hello—what's your name?' they asked, reaching out and stroking Louisa's doll at the same time.

'My name's Louisa. And yours?'

'I'm Renee' and 'I'm Maria', they answered simultaneously. 'Your doll's so nice,' they added.

'She's called Yvonne and she's from America,' said Louisa proudly. 'She's like a real baby. Look–she can open and close her eyes and you can see two teeth and a sweet little tongue through her mouth. Do you like her?'

The girls reached out for Yvonne. 'Oh yes, can we hold her?'

'Yes, of course you can. Can I have a look at your pram?'

Louisa's doll changed hands. The girls handed over the pram and their doll to her. They took and held Yvonne with great care. Maria, the younger, kissed her on her porcelain cheek. Louisa turned her attention to the pram. Suddenly, from the corner of her eye, she saw the black-and-white cat approaching very slowly, like a fashion model on a platform.

'The cat again,' said Louisa, pleased.

'Go away, go away Mamee!' screamed Renee and Maria.

'Please don't send her away–she's such a pretty cat,' begged Louisa. Her fear was forgotten since she was now surrounded by others. She liked the look of the cat, calm and elegant.

Renee became agitated. 'Oh no, no–we want her to go away. She's such a thief,' she said, looking at the cat. 'We can't leave our doors or windows open. In she comes. She takes everything. Go on, go away, go away–'

'But she's so pretty. Don't frighten her,' said Louisa. The cat ran away towards the back of the house. 'Why is she so frightened? Whose is she?" she asked.

The girls looked at each other and giggled. 'You can call her Mamee–that's what everyone calls her. She's really horrible.

She belonged to the people who used to live in your house. They left her behind. There's nobody to feed her now, so she steals. She's a real nuisance. We call her Mamee—the midwife—because the woman she belonged to was a midwife. We don't know her real name. She's only a cat, after all.'

Renee said all this in one breath, but from her almost-affectionate tone it was clear that, however naughty the cat was, it was tolerated, if not always loved.

'How could they possibly abandon her like that?" Louisa responded. 'Poor cat.'

'Oh, they left her all right. They left for the mainland on the ferryboat. Cats don't like the sea or any kind of water. This cat wouldn't have liked it over there. She was born here, so they thought she'd be happier if she were left behind. Now she's such a pain.'

'Go away, go away, stupid cat,' the girls carried on screaming. After the poor animal had disappeared again, Maria said, in a different tone of voice: 'I love your doll. Let's put her in the pram and go into my back garden. Then we can feed her through her half-open mouth.'

She beamed at Louisa. 'Let's all be friends.'

Without waiting for permission, Maria made Yvonne comfortable in the pram, stuffed her own doll on top and pushed the pram towards the gate of the house next to Louisa's. Renee and Louisa followed, holding hands.

'I live across the road, and she lives there,' explained Renee, pointing to the other two houses. 'We're first cousins and we go to the same school. Are you going to come to our school too?'

'I don't know. It hasn't been decided yet,' said Louisa.

A new home, the slaughterhouse, pea stew...

Maria's garden was shady and cool, refreshing for the little girls who were in any case youthfully stoic about the heat. The garden consisted of two terraces overlooking the sea, the boats and the islands. The bottom terrace had an iron water pump in the middle, with stone seats around it. Louisa looked at the pump with amazement. She'd never seen any such thing before.

The sea stretched before them to the mainland, deep blue and calm. Two little islands and small fishing boats could be seen in the distance. The mist caused by the humidity had lifted and there was no longer a single cloud in the sky. The three girls descended the few steps to the lower terrace and gazed out.

'Ah, this is wonderful,' said Louisa joyfully.

Forgetting the dolls, Renee and Maria shouted: 'Come on, let's go swimming right now, because tomorrow we won't be able to. Louisa, go and put your costume on and come back. We'll go straight away.'

All three immediately ran to change their clothes.

That night, Louisa went to bed happy. This new house was the best in the world, and Renee and Maria were her very best friends.

The following day she was awoken by screams, lots of screams. She could hear her father moving about in the dining room. He hadn't yet left for work. 'It must be very early,' she thought. She could hear Blossom washing clothes in the back garden.

The screaming went on. They were terrible screams which, interspersed with strange wailing, made all other sounds seem insignificant. Louisa quickly got out of bed and ran out just as she was, in her white cotton knickers and vest, through the door leading to the back garden.

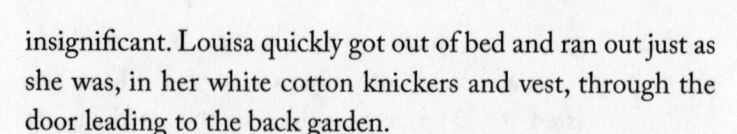

The packing cases had been removed and emptied by her father. Louisa found, entering the new territory of their garden that it had two terraces like the house next door. Louisa's new house was built on a slope leading to the main road and then to a beach. An imposing iron water pump similar to the one she had seen the day before stood on the bottom terrace.

The garden was beautiful and tranquil and apart from her stepmother washing at the pump, she could see no-one else. But the terrible sounds were becoming louder. They seemed to come from somewhere outside their garden. Louisa saw the sea spread out in front of her, the same view as from the terrace next door she had seen the day before. But this was a different sea. It wasn't blue any more but red: thick blood red. The colour didn't reach all the way across to the mainland, but halfway to the little islands. Beyond that it was blue again.

Louisa paused to consider. Everything was the same as the day before except for the screams and the wailing and the red sea. Then she saw what it was. Along the road came a huge articulated lorry, and on it were hundreds of pigs. They were crying, screaming, fighting to get off, but they couldn't, they were so tightly packed.

The lorry was heading towards a big building to the left of their house. The building was made of rusty corrugated iron, with the redeeming feature of elaborate tin lace-work attached to the guttering all the way round. Across the road, leading into the sea, Louisa could see a thick cement pipe. Blood poured from it into the water.

Louisa turned and ran to the pump where Blossom was washing the clothes. 'The sea has blood in it. Why?' she screamed.

Blossom lifted her head and said calmly and gently: 'Please don't cry again. That building over there is the municipal slaughterhouse. Every Monday, Wednesday, and Friday they slaughter animals there so that we can all eat nice, nutritious food. The animals come from all over the place: sheep, calves, pigs, cows. Don't worry. This will happen all the time. But remember: no swimming today–nor on Wednesday nor Friday.' When Louisa looked horrified, she said kindly: 'You'll get used to it.'

Louisa withdrew to the wall that marked the end of the garden. She was mesmerised; she'd never seen red sea before. The stench was sickening, and the screaming and crying of the animals filled her with despair. The previous evening's happiness had disappeared, to be replaced by a sense of fear and astonishment. She had never asked where the meat, which they ate once a week, came from.

She sat and stared at the slaughterhouse. It looked awfully busy. Men in huge overalls, once white but now covered with vast quantities of dried blood, were coming in and out to help unload the animals. The animals were resisting with all their might, hopelessly. They were ferociously pushed, and vanished inside, still screaming. If that wasn't bad enough, there was no swimming today. Louisa felt sad about the animals, but equally sad about the sea.

Then she saw Mamee the cat loitering and sniffing around the slaughterhouse. She was probably still looking for food. Now Blossom was hanging out the washing. At last Louisa retreated into the house. Her father had left for work on his bicycle. So this was Monday, the day for slaughtering animals, washing clothes and abstaining from swimming.

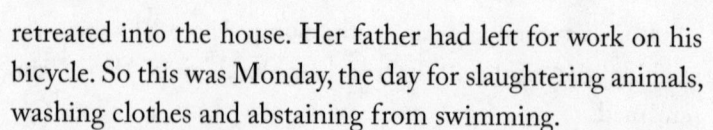

Over the next weeks, Louisa felt she had entered a new life and a new routine. But her thoughts constantly returned to the old apartment. Memories ceaselessly flooded her mind. Every morning when she awoke, she would daydream about the past. But she knew there was no way back. The old life was gone, just like her mother. How could she create a future as she would like it to be?

Life went on in Portovecchio. One day, soon after the family had settled into the new house, Louisa woke up quite late. She got out of bed and went through the hall into the dining room which had become the heart of this new house. The formal drawing room was the only room which had not yet been set up. Tony needed time to furnish it as he wanted. This was a special room, spacious and full of mock-Baroque murals on the ceiling and walls. A huge chandelier crafted with aristocratic pretensions hung in the middle of the ceiling, and the room demanded the right sort of furniture below.

The dining room, by contrast, was plain and functional. In its centre was a large round mahogany table covered with a big embroidered tablecloth. Louisa hated this product of her stepmother's labour. It had come with her, inside the trunk where she kept all the treasures of her dowry. Blossom could never part from her beloved embroidery, and this tablecloth was one of the few things that Tony let her display in their new house.

Blossom was willing to teach Louisa how to use the needle, canvas and scissors, but the girl kept turning down the offer.

A new home, the slaughterhouse, pea stew...

She would rather have somebody read her favourite book, *Robinson Crusoe*, to her, over and over again. It was the book her mother had given her before she died. In her daydreams, Louisa indulged in a precious fantasy which was stored away in a convenient corner of her brain, to be visited at special times, especially just before sleep closed her bright blue eyes. It was an escape from the dark of the night to an island far away from everywhere. The island was surrounded by turquoise sea so clear you could see the bottom, through waters full of multicoloured fish swimming about. Louisa had no concept of coral reefs. She could only dream of flat sandy seabeds, of seaweed, of an island where, left entirely on her own, she would develop Crusoe's skills in order to survive. Then she would never have any reason to leave the island.

She didn't want to belong to this family. It wasn't her family any more. Why did her father marry again? She still couldn't understand. On the island she would never need to see her father or stepmother.

The dining room of the new house had three doors and two French windows. One door led to the kitchen, one to Tony and Blossom's bedroom and one to the hall. Louisa's bedroom was across this hall, which she had to cross to enter the dining room. She never went into the main bedroom. She found that too hard, since all the furniture there was what had filled the other bedroom before her mother died. In fact, all the furniture had come from her mother's family. She knew that because her mother used to hold her by the hand and walk her around the enchanted bedroom pointing out to her things that her own mother had owned as a child, in her own room on another island further down the archipelago.

Blossom had brought no furniture to this house. She came with only her clothes, her linen dowry, her distaff for winding her wool, and bags and bags of wool ready to spin. Her new husband had forbidden her to bring her own things since he saw it as peasant furniture totally unsuitable for their new home.

On the dining room table Louisa noticed a glass of milk and a couple of biscuits left there by her stepmother. This was her breakfast. She wasn't hungry, so she walked to the kitchen through the back door, and out to the garden. Blossom was standing next to the low fence, talking to their neighbour. In the background, pumping water, was a young woman. Her movements were rhythmic and determined; the slightest pause and the water would lose its flow.

The neighbour, a lady of about thirty-five, was tall and elegant, with beautiful but sad brown eyes. She looked ethereal. Her sad expression was like a transparent veil in front of her face. Before her mother had become ill, Louisa had gone with her to the open-air cinema and had seen *Queen Christina*, with Greta Garbo and John Gilbert. This lady reminded her of Greta Garbo.

This was strange, since in her early daydreams her mother's real face had also become Greta Garbo's. These days, hard as she tried, Louisa couldn't form her mother's real image in her mind. Her mother had become faceless.

This new Queen Christina was Maria's mother. Louisa's new friend was standing next to her, embracing her round her hips, clinging to her with adoration. Maria looked totally comfortable in that position. Her mother was also relaxed, in spite of her blank expression.

'This is my mum,' Maria said. 'She's called Zoë. What's your mum called?'

Louisa felt a lump form in her throat. Her mum had been called Poppy. The woman standing next to her now *was not* her mother. She had been told by Tony to call her 'Mum', but she found it difficult even to refer to her by that precious name. But she couldn't bring herself to explain to Maria about the mother she'd lost; she couldn't tell her that the woman standing there was not related to her and never would be. She couldn't put into words the fact that she'd been left motherless, and that her father had married again, to this utterly irrelevant woman who nevertheless wanted to cuddle her and love her.

Louisa was overwhelmed by a deep sense of shame for being an orphan and having a stepmother from a region far from her mother's family home. She was also ashamed that she came with relatives who looked different, spoke differently, behaved differently.

Louisa clenched her teeth and indicated her stepmother. 'She's called Blossom,' was all she said. Then she went and sat on the doorstep.

The conversation between Blossom and Zoë was lively, even though the women were very different. Their accents indicated that they came from different regions. Their clothes were of different styles. Blossom was in fact dressed without style or taste. Her clothes were in good condition, but they were work clothes. Zoë was dressed in a black dress with long sleeves; only a tiny collar edged with a little lace relieved the severity of her appearance. The dress was clean and well pressed. Since a maid was doing the washing behind her at the water pump, Zoë didn't wear an apron.

Louisa observed the black dress, and wondered who had died in this family–but she didn't dare ask.

The women's conversation was about the cat. Zoë was repeating the story of Mamee. 'You must keep your doors closed at all times,' she was saying. 'This wretched cat plagues us. I don't know what we can do. She's good-looking, but a real nuisance. I don't dare leave the kitchen door open. She creeps in and jumps everywhere.'

It was as if she were a mother talking about her naughty but adorable child. Deep down, Zoë loved the cat, and felt sorry she had been abandoned. Stroking the animal comforted and calmed her. But she also had to pretend, like everybody else in the neighbourhood, that she found her a nuisance.

'Oh poor thing…' Blossom kept repeating. Her conversational skills were limited to cooking and trivialities. Debating a cat's predicament was not an important concern.

'I'd better go back to the kitchen,' she added. 'I'm going to cook peas with potatoes.'

Zoë was curious. 'How do you do that?'

'This is the best season for this dish,' Blossom said. '*He* went to the market yesterday and bought fresh peas and lots of dill– and this is what he ordered.'

Blossom had found it impossible, since she'd found herself married to Louisa's father, to call Tony by his name, or even to refer to him as 'Tony' or 'my husband'. She always referred to 'he' or 'him'. Her husband seemed as foreign to her as an alien from Outer Space. They may have shared the same language and the same bed, but that is as far as it went.

'You need fresh onions too,' Blossom continued. 'You shell the peas and wash them well. I can never resist eating some while I shell them. You grate the onion, and then you take five medium-sized potatoes for the three of us. You peel and quarter them, take a bunch of dill, wash it and chop it up. You add olive oil, salt and pepper. You put them all in your heavy-bottomed saucepan. You light the paraffin stove…'

'Oh, we have a gas stove,' said Zoë with pride, 'but I don't actually do the cooking.'

Louisa lowered her head and rested it on her bended knees. How embarrassing! Her family must be the only one left using a paraffin stove. Gas stoves had come into use after her mother's death, but nobody had thought of updating their kitchen. Blossom was of country stock and actually enjoyed acting the peasant in this town household.

'Theodora–listen,' said Zoë, turning to the girl at the pump. Then she addressed Blossom again: 'She's our maid. She lives up the road, and she's been working for me since she was fifteen. She's seventeen now.' Theodora gave them all a sullen look, but didn't utter a word.

Louisa thought how elegant her mother had been. She had only rarely gone into the kitchen. There was a maid to do all the family's housework, and they had also employed a man who ran all the household errands. He never wore shoes. Now they had disappeared, with her mother… her hats, her beautiful dresses. They would never again see all those people who used to visit them at their apartment, as friends. All that was over. This new life with a grumpy father and a strange woman was so different. The three of them struggled to meet but the mental distance between them was wider than the Vikos Gorge.

Blossom was, meanwhile, unstoppable. 'You take a shallow saucepan. Heat the oil, add the onion and the quartered potatoes, fry gently for a few minutes, and then add the fresh peas and enough water to cover them. Add salt and pepper. Towards the end you add the fresh dill. Put on a lid and simmer slowly until the potatoes and peas are cooked. You can eat the dish hot or cold, with brown bread and lettuce salad with lots of oregano and chopped cheese, oil and vinegar. You couldn't have a better meal.'

She was clearly inspired by her description. 'Off I go,' she said. 'Bye for now,' as if she'd had enough of chitchat. The prospect of cooking the most delicious peas in the Hellenic Kingdom was much more attractive.

Suddenly she turned and, addressing Zoë, who was still standing with Maria, said firmly and abruptly: 'Louisa must never again go swimming with your girls in this sea. How can you let them swim in this filthy water? He—and he's a very intelligent man who knows everything—has forbidden it. He nearly killed me when he heard that they had gone swimming. This sea is filthy and the beach is muddy and covered with what's left over from the animals.'

Then she turned again and walked away. Louisa went red, and couldn't look at her friend. Slowly she followed her stepmother indoors to have her breakfast. If she left it too long, she would spoil her appetite for family lunch and Blossom's pea stew would be wasted.

She was devastated. Why would Maria want her as a friend after Blossom's abruptness? She ran into the dining room and looked for her breakfast. But on the table there was only a little puddle of milk. The glass had smashed to the floor, and the plate with the biscuits had been knocked over on to the chair beside the table.

'Mamma, come quick! Mamee's been here,' Louisa found herself calling.

Blossom entered the dining room screaming. Nothing made her madder than losing food, wasting it or throwing it away.

'Ah, the horrible cat, the bastard, the impostor!' she yelled. 'I'm going to show her. It's all your fault,' she said, immediately blaming Louisa. 'You left the door open. And didn't I tell you to drink your milk as soon as you get out of bed? I shall tell your father everything.'

Louisa turned and ran out to the garden. Attached to the back of the house was a shed. She escaped into it, closing the door behind her.

The family had been absolutely delighted when they found the house had a shed.

'I can do my washing there in winter,' said Blossom.

'Oh no you can't: this is a special place for Louisa,' said Tony. 'I'll do it up so she can play in here with her dolls and her friends.' He had spoken aggressively and authoritatively.

He always reproached Blossom with contempt and anger. Louisa was embarrassed by this behaviour. In spite of her constant feeling of unease towards this woman, she hated her father for being so hard on her. After all, he was the one who had had the brilliant idea of marrying again.

With Blossom's reluctant help, Tony had transformed the shed into a cosy mini-apartment for Louisa. Her doll's pram and bed were put in there, her little armchair, and all her books and toys. A corner was dedicated to little toy kitchen items. A mat was placed on the cement flooring for her to sleep on. A miniature sitting room was set up in another corner for her to entertain her friends, with the cutest little window looking out to the garden, draped with white lace curtains. Louisa was delighted.

As soon as her den had been set up, she started using it. At night she would sleep in her bedroom in the proper house, but during the day–since it was the summer holidays–she would spend her time in the cool of her den. She would get up early and disappear there for most of the day. In this place of her own Louisa found a safe haven when she was distressed.

And she *was* distressed by much of what Blossom did. She hated all this talk about cooking, and she hated Blossom's abruptness over the swimming issue.

When she entered her den one day, she closed the door behind her and saw Mamee curled up in the middle of her mat. They looked at each other. Louisa remained still so as not to frighten the cat. After gazing indifferently at her, the cat got up and walked in her fashion-model way towards the door. Since it was closed, she started circling around inside the den, then returned to the mat, lay down and carried on staring at Louisa.

Louisa went and sat in her little armchair. It was a hot, still day, and even the coolness of the den didn't make her feel better. They kept staring at one another, the cat curled up on the mat, Louisa in her armchair. After a few minutes Louisa got up, took her swimming costume down from its hook, put it on and ran down to the beach and into the blue water.

The cat chased her half-way down the hill, then disappeared behind a bush. The blue sea sparkled in the sunshine. The slaughterhouse was not working that day.

Louisa had made up her mind. She was not going to obey her father's rule.

Nobody else was on the beach as she walked slowly into the water. She could see the bottom, but her feet, instead of touching solid sand, sank into soft oozing mud. She persevered. She had expected it to be like this, just as it had been the first day she swam with the girls. The ooze had to do with the waste matter from the slaughterhouse. The girls had encouraged her to stay because the quality of sea and sand improved further away from the shore.

That's what she did on this day. She went out until the water came to her waist and then she plunged in and swam. Her mother had loved the sea and had taught her to swim. Louisa swam on and on until she was out of her depth. Blossom, still busy in the kitchen, had no idea what she was up to.

At last, tired, Louisa made her way back in, left the water, climbed the slope and hid in her den. She changed her clothes, lay down on her mat, took up her beloved *Robinson Crusoe* and started reading. She could still smell the sea on her body and licked the salt from her arms.

Her mind could not have been further from Blossom and her stepmother's preoccupations. 'What are we going to eat today?' was the first question Blossom asked every day as soon as she left the bedroom. Without hesitation her husband would dictate a menu. 'Fish, today,' he would order. Then he would ask Louisa to go with him to meet the fishermen returning with their full nets.

If it was slaughterhouse day, the road at the back of the house would be manically busy. Tony would open the back gate and both of them go down the steps to where all the commotion with the animals was going on.

One day her father greeted an elderly man in a dark suit, carrying a little briefcase and walking towards the slaughterhouse. He didn't look as if he came from Portovecchio, so Louisa assumed that he must have come from the town.

'Good morning, Mr Mizrahi,' said Tony.

'Good morning to you, too,' the man replied, with a heavy accent.

'We're having fish today, Mr Mizrahi.'

'That's a good idea. Where are you getting it from?'

'From over there.' And Tony pointed towards the little jetty where Zoë with Maria, and Renee with her mother Joy were standing looking into a blue, yellow and white boat.

'The fishermen have arrived,' called Louisa.

'Can you buy some for me? I'm on my way to the slaughterhouse, and I can't delay any longer. I'd be so grateful,' Mr Mizrahi said.

'Yes, of course—what would you like?'

'A medium-sized snapper, if there is one. I'll give you the money as soon as I finish in there.'

'Consider it done.'

'Dad, who was that man? I've never seen him before,' Louisa asked as they crossed the road to the shore.

'He's the Rabbi,' Tony replied. 'The Jewish priest.'

'Why is he going to the slaughterhouse?'

Tony explained, as briefly as he could, how necessary it was for the Rabbi to visit the slaughterhouse so he could supervise the slaughter of animals for the local Jewish community to eat. His special little knife touched no pigs, of course, he added.

Louisa was puzzled; she'd never heard of anything like this before. But nor had she ever thought about slaughterhouses, either. Everything happening around her in Portovecchio was new, different. Sometimes it all seemed too enormous for her young life.

As they approached the jetty, she read aloud the name of the boat: *Alice*. Inside there were two men, obviously father and son, since they looked so alike, although one was old. Both of them were deeply tanned, their shoulders the colour of dark gold. Their hair was blond, so blond that it shone in the sun, reminding Louisa of her doll's fake hair.

The women with their daughters saw Tony approaching with Louisa. Turning to the fishermen, they said: 'Let's hope you have enough for all of us.'

The fishermen were reassuring. 'Don't worry. There's enough even for the cats.'

At this moment Mamee reappeared. She looked supremely confident, and ignored everyone. The older fisherman grabbed a handful of sardines from the nets and threw them on to the jetty, towards her.

'Let her eat,' the two women said to one another. 'If she fills up here, she might keep away from our kitchens.'

The fishermen's boat was rocking slowly in the ruby-coloured sea. The slaughterhouse had been pouring blood out into the water for a couple of hours. The two men were discarding the small, good-for-nothing tiny fish into the bloody water.

Louisa stared at them, but couldn't think of anything to say. Her life had become a parody of *Alice in Wonderland*. Her body was in Portovecchio but her little soul was far away with her friends and their games in the town. She was also thinking of Robinson Crusoe and how he would have fished and cooked. If these two fishmermen were blonds, her Robinson would have become almost as dark as his Man Friday, she imagined.

The young fisherman wore a pair of trousers that reached just below his strong knees, no shoes and no shirt. He must have been in the water, because his trousers were wet and clung to his body. The salt created white trickling veins on his golden body. 'He must taste very salty,' Louisa thought, scrutinising him some more. His eyes were the colour of the sea on a clear day, and he was clean-shaven. He was sorting through the fish with great confidence.

The fishermen usually went out in the evenings, returning to the island the following morning. The older man was now busy organising orders for the waiting customers. He was wearing torn blue jeans and around his neck hung a sacred talisman of the sort purchased by most local people from the priests of St Spiridion. They sold them at the church. They were little pieces of cloth from St Spiridion's slipper, wrapped in a tiny beaded case. People hung them from a row of beads around their necks.

'I need half a kilo of scorpion fish,' Tony said. 'We're having fish stew today. I also need a snapper for the Rabbi.'

'Anything you want,' the old fisherman replied. Mamee kept licking and chewing the fish bones.

'She's so hungry,' the son remarked.

'You're such a softie,' his father said, laughingly. To the others he said: 'He misses his girlfriend.' Turning to the boy, he winked and added seriously: 'Don't you?'

'What's his girlfriend got to do with the cat?' Tony asked.

'The midwife, the one who lived in your house before you arrived, has a daughter. The son had taken a fancy to her– but now they've all gone. Only the cat is left,' said Renee's mother, Joy. This was for Tony's information.

Louisa thought the boy had tears in his eyes–but it could have been seawater. He jumped quickly out of the boat on to the jetty with the cat. She didn't acknowledge him. She simply lay down on the hot concrete of the jetty and let him stroke her. Louisa couldn't resist joining in. She approached and stroked the cat's stomach.

Tony wasn't having any of this. He shouted: 'Get away, old cat! You're so filthy, the sooner you disappear the better.' But the cat reminded Louisa of her life in Athens, of the time she'd spent with Aunt Camilla's pampered pet.

With a leap, the young fisherman got back on the boat. Louisa picked up the two plastic bags of fish, one for Mr Mizrahi and one for them. The adults paid. Then they all started back towards their houses. The fish shopping was complete.

Blossom received the fish with delight, although she was dreading the cleaning. Scorpions' bones or fins could be dangerous if they happened to prick you when you cleaned them, so she scaled and washed them very carefully. Then she put the fish on a big white platter. Onions again. She couldn't think of many dishes in which onions were not a must. She'd peeled hundreds of thousands of onions over the years.

She had asked her brother George to bring them from the village every time he came to visit. He brought a mixture of red and white ones, in a huge wide-brimmed basket covered with a rough cloth. His wife securely sewed a cover around the edge of the basket so that the onions wouldn't escape on the bus.

Blossom now had an unlimited supply of onions. Sometimes she'd just eat them as a snack: a thick slice of fresh, hot brown bread straight from the local bakery, sprinkled with lots of olive oil, covered with a good spread of tomato paste. She would eat it with a peeled onion on the side—a bite of bread, a bite of onion. So delicious!

Today she needed white onions. 'He' had bought three small-to-medium scorpion fish, bright red in colour, with huge wide-open eyes. Their prickly skin and fangs protruded in all directions, deadly. Blossom took a deep saucepan, put it on the stove, lit it and warmed a little olive oil. Then she added two finely grated onions, lots of chopped-up garlic, two sliced carrots and a little sliced celery. She sautéed them slightly, and when the vegetables became soft and a little brown, took the saucepan away from the heat. Then she added the fish and enough water to cover it. She sprinkled the stew with plenty of salt and pepper, enough cayenne pepper and paprika to turn it a deep red colour and then added two bay leaves. She replaced the saucepan on top of the stove and boiled everything very slowly for about ten minutes.

Soon the delicious fish stew was ready for lunch. They would not eat before three o'clock in the afternoon, but the cooking had been done, and so she could get on with the rest of her housework.

Tony had mounted his bike and left for work.

Mr Mizrahi called on Blossom to collect his snapper without entering the house. He turned down her offer of a cup of coffee or a glass of water. He took the fish and thanked her, remarking that her fish stew smelled delicious. He declined the offer of a spoonful 'just for the road'. Louisa thought him arrogant and unfriendly: why wouldn't he accept their food? Wasn't he ever hungry or thirsty?

Louisa was beginning to love her new environment. Their back garden was the best of all in the row of houses. It had the biggest number of fruit trees and rose bushes, of all colours. They gave off the most beautiful, fragrant smell. Louisa liked one in particular, a bush that produced enormous yellow roses with just a faint touch of pink. The smell was heavenly. This bush dominated the lower terrace and Louisa discovered a little bench next to it which she started to use so that she could enjoy the sea view.

If life could be sad and miserable without her mother, this landscape gave her a feeling of joy. It was like entering the Garden of Eden. Her teacher at her old school had been describing the Garden in Religious Studies, calling it the best place in the whole world. Louisa's Garden of Eden was also Robinson Crusoe's island, but with roses and deep blue sea all around.

Admittedly, here one day the sea was blue and the next red, but even when it was bloody, the whole view was stunning. Opposite her were two small islands, and some large rocks, all appearing to float on the calm water. The rocks and islands were green, covered in bushes and tall, thin cypress trees.

Louisa had never visited these islands. She knew they were out of bounds. The bigger of the two, Vido, was a juvenile prison, the fear and horror of all the youth in Kerkyra. The other, Lazaretto, was even worse. It was the island of execution.

From the land you could vaguely see the Wall of Execution among the cypress trees. You could just make out a grey wall in the distance; in some parts greenery could be seen where creepers were taking over.

Beyond there were high mountains. Sometimes these appeared blue; at other times, especially at sunset, they turned a vibrant pink. Most of these mountains belonged to another country, Albania, and couldn't be visited.

She suddenly realised that this was no longer a Robinson Crusoe landscape. It was real, full of living people. She knew that life in Albania was one of poverty, of bare survival, and on Lazaretto her fellow Greeks were shooting the Communists. Just a couple of miles away, across the sea, the Albanian Communists were imprisoning and executing non-Communists, she had heard the adults say. What *is* a Communist, anyway? Louisa wondered.

Boats continually came and went. The island's harbour was close, and the pattern was that ships would arrive very early in the morning and then leave by eleven o'clock. To the left of their house lay Maria's house and garden, and beyond that the slaughterhouse. On the opposite side was the priest's house, and beyond that, after the church, lived the fisherman with his family. From it came the two men from whom they had bought their fish. Next to the shore was a small shipyard where lots of little fishing boats were resting lopsidedly, waiting for repair. Others were moored by the jetty.

Louisa grew to love watching the men at work repairing the boats, and the fishermen going in and out.

While she was sitting peacefully, she saw that Mamee was approaching. She called her the way any little girl would call a cat. 'Come on, little one—come to me. I'm not scared of you any more. Come on, let's be friends. I was a good friend of your sister in Athens,' she called. The cat approached Louisa slowly. Then she jumped on to the bench and sat comfortably next to her.

Louisa started stroking and talking to her. She told her all the gossip she'd heard around and about and reassured her that she would look after her. She would feed her—never mind about her previous owners. She'd make sure that she would never go without food. They would be friends.

Then she found herself telling the cat that once upon a time there was a woman called Poppy, who was very pretty, with dark brown hair and eyes. She used to wear a straw hat with a huge brim in the summer. She would wear flowing, flowery dresses and take Louisa by the hand for long walks.

Louisa couldn't tell the cat that this woman had been her mother. She said only that she was now gone forever and wasn't going to come back. 'Just like your owners, little one,' she told the cat.

At lunchtime her father returned from work on his bike. He was looking forward to his spicy fish stew. Instead he found Blossom cursing. On the table there was only tomato salad, salted sardines in oil and vinegar and fresh brown bread.

'Where's the fish?' he demanded.

'That cursed Mamee grabbed it from the platter and spoiled it all while I was laying the table,' Blossom answered angrily.

Tony became enraged and started yelling. He blamed Blossom, the cat, and the real Mamee/midwife who'd abandoned her cat when she left. The ferocity of his threats astonished little Louisa. Why was her father always so angry, so enraged? The days of calm domestic bliss had vanished with the death of her mother.

After this incident, Louisa secretly started pouring lots of milk into a plastic container, originally her doll's plate. Then she would add stale bread and take it to her den to feed Mamee in secret. They became the best of friends. The den was the place where they both ran when they needed to escape and find solace. The cat would curl up on the girl's lap, and Louisa would stroke her luxuriously rich black-and-white coat, touching the little bell hanging round her neck and making it sound like a magic chime from another world.

Chapter 5

Reminders of an execution, and the procession that brings together innocent souls and sinners

The good ship Achilleas
*Will take us to that isle
Some summer dawn.*

August 1956

Every year, some time on the late afternoon of 14 August (and only then), Zoë would take out of her drawer the last letter sent to her by John, her husband. It had been written on the day before his execution. Reading it always wrenched her heart. She followed the words through thick salty tears.

Next to her bed stood a small table, which John had painted pink just before they married. Pink had always been her favourite colour, baby pink in particular. She had wanted everything in her new marital bedroom to be that colour. John's abrupt departure had, however, left the room unfinished. Only one bedside table was pink. The other remained raw plywood which was slowly but steadily going mouldy.

Zoë kept her letter under lock and key, in the drawer of the pink table just a few inches from her pillow. The drawer was lined with silky white paper that had little pink roses printed on it. It contained an empty perfume bottle, a name day present that John had given her. The scent had long since been used, but she kept the bottle. Every night she went to sleep thinking of John, until unconsciousness took over. With the letter safe by her bedside, she felt a sense of comfort. To her, in spite of its associations of misery, it was part of her lost husband. It kept his aura in the house with her.

John had been executed sometime around 15 August 1949. Zoë wasn't sure exactly when. Nobody had ever given her a death certificate. She had merely been handed a typed letter announcing her husband's death by firing squad.

'They' were evil, but could they really have committed such an act on a holy day, the day of the Assumption of the Virgin Mary, the feast commemorating her journey to Heaven? 'They' professed themselves good Christians, after all. Zoë had received the letter on 16 August, the day after her daughter Maria was born. She had still been in bed, the tiny baby in a cot by her side. Since then, on 14 August every year, after all her housework had been done, Zoë left the house dressed formally, as if for church. Everything was spotlessly clean: the garden walls and the trunks of the trees whitewashed; the beds freshly changed; the brass and silver transformed into warmly glowing objects; the mahogany furniture polished to a high shine with olive oil and vinegar. Her body had been washed with warm soapy water, and her thick, silky jet-black hair rinsed with red wine vinegar and carefully combed. She carried with her the precious letter.

Such meticulous preparation of house and body also had another purpose. Every 15 August, the entire population of

Portovecchio gathers at its highest point to commemorate and venerate the Virgin Mary. Since it has its own special little church in Her honour, it holds two days of feasting.

August 15 was not just the day when John had disappeared forever. It was also little Maria's name day and birthday. Every year when Zoë took out the letter to read, she remembered that on 15 August 1949, around six, while she was running to the outhouse because her waters had broken, she had heard shots coming from Lazaretto. For a few seconds she had wondered whose turn had come, but her labour pains had distracted her. She didn't think for a moment that, only two miles away, her husband had slumped to the ground, dead.

Since 1947 early morning shots had become a regular feature of the island's life. The government had decided that as many Communists as possible were to be eliminated 'for the safety of the country'. Had the accused really done anything wrong? Had they conspired to take anybody's life? Had they really killed anyone? Or did they have to go because of their dangerous and harmful ideology? People were left wondering.

The executions always took place at dawn, presumably so that nobody would notice, across the water on Kerkyra. But most people were awake early enough to hear the firing. Some, like the factory workers, builders and labourers were already on their way to work, while the fishermen had been up and working for hours. All these men had the energy drawn out of their bodies every day in exchange for the bare means of survival and support for themselves and the families they had created. Others, who made their way to work later, and in a more leisurely way, usually received greater rewards. Their seldom-expressed concern for the poor was purely theoretical, a fruitless topic of idle conversation. At least, that's what the Communists of the time argued in their discussions of social injustice in impoverished Hellas.

It was always the labourers who announced that there had been more executions. But like everybody else, they shrugged their shoulders and cursed the situation in which they found themselves.

After John was arrested, Zoë suffered from terrible insomnia. She would think of him in his cell, all on his own–or was he in a shared cell? She had tried to imagine what kind of food he ate every day. Bean soup, perhaps, which he hated. In Zoë's innocent understanding there was no room for thoughts of torture. She couldn't imagine John being tortured. In her ignorance and naïve goodness she didn't know that this is what people do to one another to show their power or strength, or to obtain a confession.

What little political education she had been given came about through John's enthusiasm and fervour for the doctrines of Communism. Of course World War II had tormented them both. She had never understood why there was such turmoil. Portovecchio was only a patch of insignificant ground in the context of the sweep of world history. Certainly, the Old Town had been devastated–but Zoë never went to town. Her house, her little garden, John and the view of the sea were her whole world.

So she worried about what she knew. Had John lost weight? His body had always been delicate. And he had been such a kind, gentle man. He had always told the truth during his short life. He had never harmed anyone. He had a constantly smiling face and a kind word for everyone, except for the rich, powerful and ruthless. He had loved his books and kept extensive notes.

Zoë could still feel his lips on her mouth. She was the only one in the world who really remembered his physical presence. She knew the essence of her husband would go with her to her grave.

Her daughter had of course never known her father. His own mother, who lived with them, never talked about him. To the old woman, he was still associated with the smell and feel of a baby. To Zoë he was forever a friend, a lover. Without him she felt mutilated, bereft. She assumed her mother-in-law was also hurting. But she never cried—at least not in front of Zoë. She maintained a stern look on her face. Zoë sometimes thought that she was more angry than sad at what had happened. Neither could comfort the other in a physical or an emotional way. Their language of communication consisted of requests and orders.

Their pain differed not only because of the relationship each had built with John but also because of their age. His mother was old; she was more or less on her way out of this world so she'd come to accept death. Zoë was young and her body still felt John's touch. Before he died, she would wake up at three in the morning, alert to the sounds of machine guns. She would remain in agony until a letter arrived from him, telling her that he was still alive.

The delivery of Maria took place about midday on the 15 August, on Zoë's own brass bed, the bed where the baby had been conceived and where John had slept on the night of his arrest. It was the bed on which they had made love for the first time; it was also the bed on which her own father had died. It was huge and solid, made of brass. It had belonged to someone important: Elisabeth of Austria or Kaiser Wilhelm of Germany—who now knew? Long after Elisabeth had left Kerkyra and the Kaiser had gone into exile, the Hellenic government had sold most of the furniture from the Achilleion, the fairy-tale palace 'worthy of Achilles' which had been purchased by the Kaiser.

Zoë's father, with a weak spot for royalty and the aristocracy, had bought the bed in an auction the municipality had organised. The elaborate brass bedstead was made up of huge intertwined bunches of grapes, cherries and mythological eagles. The Tree of Life was at its centre, and tiny doves rested on its branches. An imperial crest sat on the top branch. Although she had no idea what any of this meant, Zoë loved the bed. It went well with her pink dream world and made her feel like a princess, especially when she lay in it with John by her side.

The maid hated the bed. She had to polish the whole thing three times a year, and the smell of Brasso clogged her sinuses for days on end. John was ambivalent about it, and used to joke: 'Can you imagine, a Communist sleeping on an Imperial bed? This is how it is in the Soviet Union now. Off with the rich and the unjust! Time for *us* to sleep in a bit of comfort.' Then he would turn towards her and kiss her softly, as the bed creaked all over. 'Hush, be quiet,' Zoë would whisper. 'Your mother will hear us.'

Was John really killed just because he wanted a little bit of comfort? she wondered.

On 15 August 1949, her mother-in-law acted as midwife as little Maria had entered the world. Why do innocent babies come into this dreadful world? Zoë often asked herself. It was far from being a decent place, she thought. Why inflict its trials and sorrows on someone created from pure love? Wasn't that a sin in itself? But if people were to stop having babies, then what?

Brought low by unrecognised, undiagnosed depression, Zoë had felt she couldn't justify anything any more. Maybe one day she would understand, would move beyond the futility of it all. Didn't her name mean 'life'?

On this 14 August, she took the letter and walked out into the garden. She sat down by the water pump, resting her body on the marble seat. A lemon tree provided cool shade. She looked across at the tiny green island. She could just see the ruins of the old Lazaretto, and vaguely make out the Wall of Execution. They had been buried there, the Communists, every single one of them. That's all she knew: no more, no less.

Rumours swirled around. They had it that the prisoners were executed with their faces to the wall, tied to it by their iron handcuffs. They received the bullets in their backs, their faces turned away from the firing squad. Father Anthony had confirmed this. Was he telling the truth? How could she possibly know? She had also been told that after they died, the handcuffs were pulled roughly from their wrists and washed in the sea, to be used again and again.

For nearly seven months after John's arrest, she had prayed hard that 'They' would let him come back. She constantly remembered how the men had pulled him from his bed that morning and dragged him to a van parked outside. He had left wearing his blue-and-white striped pyjamas, a white vest and no shoes. She had sent him some clothes later. They at least had the grace to give them to him.

Regularly, John sent her letters. They were censored, and she read them with difficulty. She had asked him to write in big characters separated from one another, not joined together. Her schooling had been limited and cursive writing was well beyond her. He complied, and she read these precious letters time and time again until she had learned them by heart. She nearly went mad at this time through worry, since she couldn't discuss her situation with anybody. Everybody shunned her. She had become *persona non grata* overnight, the wife of a Communist prisoner. Her shadow was followed by whispers. When they realised she was pregnant, many people pitied her.

Father Anthony was the only one who had been kind. He had visited her often. Because of his position in the prison system, he could fill her in on all the gory details of Lazaretto. She often wished he wouldn't, in spite of being thirsty for news. He had been friends with both her and John, but now that her husband was gone, she resented the priest for being alive.

During her pregnancy she had prayed and prayed on her knees, before the icon of the Virgin, that John would come back. After his execution and the birth of Maria she prayed selfishly, for her own death. She was too grief-stricken to consider the implications of leaving Maria an orphan. She wished to be dead and buried deep in the centre of the earth so it would block every hole in her body and protect her from the dreadful world outside.

Father Anthony had told her, during confession, that suicidal thoughts were sinful, and had tried many times to hold her soft hand inside his own to comfort her. She always pulled away, politely.

On this evening, the sun had nearly set and the moon had just appeared on the horizon. The sea was deep blue and calm, with no reflections. A few little rowing boats were gliding by, carrying people after a day they had spent out swimming. She sat carefully on the cold marble seat, in her clean black silk dress with the little white lace collar. She was barefoot, and splashed mindlessly in the little puddle under the water pump. Since she had received this letter–nearly eight, or was it seven years ago? She couldn't count any more–she'd worn nothing but black. Her soft black hair was held back away from her face and tied up in a thick bun at the nape of her neck. She sat holding the open envelope as if the letter were a holy relic. She found it difficult to take her eyes away from Lazaretto, much as she would have liked to see it vanish forever. It was floating innocently on the Ionian Sea like all the other islands, beautiful, green and ragged.

In the garden, the sound of cicadas was relentless. Very faintly she could hear the splashing of the oars of the little boats. She could see and hear the children playing and singing. Yet everything seemed dead.

Zoë thought that she actually preferred the slaughterhouse to be in action. Its hustle and bustle kept her alert, as people hurried by, participating in life, in spite of the coming death of the animals. The sea, she thought, should be red forever, not with the blood from the animals but with that from Lazaretto, the blood of all the men sacrificed 'for the good of the country'. What could be nobler than that?

She sat quite still, breathing in the fresh scents from the jasmine bush, the lemon tree, the honeysuckle and the seaweed. *Achilleas*, the ship carrying the prisoners, must have passed close to this spot. She imagined it sliding quickly and smoothly through the bloody crimson sea, leaving a thicker wake of blood behind it. It wouldn't have been like that, though, if the execution had taken place the following day. On the feast of the Virgin Mary, you don't kill people or animals, do you?

Suddenly she started in fright. The bushes nearby were rustling. She turned round. But it was only Mamee the cat. She jumped through the bushes and on to Zoë's lap, curling up, wrinkling the silk of her dress. Zoë smiled through her tears. She welcomed the cat's company. Could the animal feel her pain? At least she couldn't advise her to stop crying, to try to forget. 'Poor thing,' she said out loud–meaning the cat. Not many people in the neighbourhood cared for her. Some fed her, others kicked her away, but somehow she had managed to put on weight. She walked around defiantly, often with an air of hostility.

Zoë had observed that her neighbour's little girl, Louisa, had taken to the cat and looked out for her. Blossom and Tony, by contrast, hated her. Perhaps they couldn't feel at home with a cat around that claimed their ground as hers. Father Anthony fed her *savouro*, and the fishermen threw leftover fish to her. Sometimes she took it, but at other times she rejected it. It all depended on how many delicacies she'd stolen that day.

As soon as the cat had settled herself, Zoë slowly stroked her smooth coat and kissed her head. Mamee seemed to be enjoying the human contact, and rested comfortably on the lap of this sad woman.

Zoë pulled John's letter out of its torn envelope and started reading, slowly:

14 August 1949
My dearest beautiful Zoë
I'm writing this from my miserable tiny cell. It's dawn, but the sun must have come up, because there's light coming through the barred hole they call a window. It's been so damp here that my bones ache. I can't imagine any more how it is outside in the middle of August.

I'm sitting on the cold flagstones underneath the window. I wish that I didn't have to write this letter. But I must.

I know that my mother tried hard to get me out of here. Promises that you and she might have been given, regarding my possible release, were endless lies. These efforts have achieved nothing. I have refused to succumb to their demands for pathetic confessions. Now you must know: by the time you receive this, I shall not exist any more. I know my end is coming.

I have always loved you more than anything in this world. Your face, your shining hair, your brown eyes, your voice are here within my heart, and they will accompany me to the end. This is my last letter to you and a farewell, forever. Tomorrow or the day after, they're going to take us on the Achilleas *to Lazaretto. Nothing will change their minds. It's 'for the good of the country', they say.*

Farewell my angel, love of my life. Death is inevitable–at least I know this much. We should be prepared and not lament it. Death is as certain as breathing. But when we know that our time is approaching, the knowledge torments us.

Please, please, please be brave and do not be hurt. Be proud of me and have faith in what I've told you. There must be a better world in the future. I shall go to my execution knowing that I have done some good for my country. I know WE are right.

I've never been a believer, you know that. Do you remember how angry Anthony used to get about my doubts? Do you remember how cross you were with my endless jokes? Perhaps you were both right. Perhaps this is my punishment for my atheism, and nothing to do with my politics. But even Jesus Christ went to the Cross for his beliefs. Why not others?

I know that you are a true Christian. You love Jesus and His Mother. Please continue to love them, and me. Think of Him and the Virgin Mary, their suffering and ours. Please.

Has our little baby been born yet? You said it was due in the middle of August. I've sent you so many letters but I haven't received many from you, my darling. I know you find writing difficult. [The censor intervened here...] *told me that no letter has arrived for some time now. But I hope you keep well and sane during this turmoil. If our baby is a girl, name her Maria. I like that name very much. It will commemorate the day that I departed this life. Please, if possible, don't wear black, but if my mother insists, do it for her sake.*

The prison is horrible, but less crowded than it used to be. Father Anthony must have told you what they do to Communists like us. ['Quite right too' the censor had added...] *I have the feeling that I'm not going to be here for very long now. The* [censored] *might transport me on the* Achilleas *soon.*

You must be brave for the sake of our child and my mother. I'm not really afraid, just sad. I love you. Please don't be angry with me. I've done nothing criminal. In our country now you get killed for ideals, not just deeds. I still don't know how they discovered my views. I'm not ashamed of them. Who betrayed me? They call me evil here, but I haven't hurt anybody in this life. I've asserted my innocence over and over again, but nobody believes me.

Zoë, I'm doomed. You might as well know it. Anthony whispered to me that the boat would soon take us to Lazaretto. Can you imagine if we sail through the bloody sea of the slaughterhouse? We're like the pigs that are slaughtered below our house. I never felt sorry for them, since they provided us with tasty meals. Is anybody going to cry for me, apart from you, my darling? My mother's angry with me, I'm told by Anthony. She told him to tell me to sign a confession. But I've nothing left but my integrity. However much I love you both, I can't do it. I've done nothing wrong. Please believe me and forgive me.

Remember that I adore you, that I'm taking your image with me to my cold, damp grave. How long is it going to take before your memory—and I—turn to dust?

My purpose has always been to better our lives here in this world, so please do what you can in your own way. My mother will stand by you, especially financially. Her property and income can't be touched by their wicked machinations. Love our child, as I am sure you will, and sometimes sit in our garden in the evenings and look across at the beautiful island of Lazaretto, where we used to go swimming and fishing in the old days, and think of me. You might imagine that I have betrayed you, but please don't let thoughts like this interfere with your love for me. You always knew what I believed. Sometimes when the cell seemed especially dark and damp, and homesickness settled in my heart, I thought of giving in to their demands. But had I done that I would have betrayed myself, everybody else, and you besides. You know that since we started all this there was no way back. What we all want is equality for everyone, free health care, free education and an end to foreign interference. Every night since they brought me here, while lying on this miserable floor, I have transported myself to our house in

Portovecchio, and thought of you only a few miles away from me. I think of your beautiful eyes. I have loved you since we were children. I have never loved any other woman in my life. I spend every night imagining us both in the kitchen, cooking or pumping water with our old pump. I think of us pushing a pram, but most of the time I think of the irony of our own dreams. Do you remember the time we were sunbathing on the white pebble beach of Lazaretto and we joked that it would be the perfect place to die together? Someone must have heard our loving whispers; the only thing is they didn't hear properly. So I shall die there on my own.

Dearest Zoë, there is a big favour I need from you. Please take care of my mother. Continue to live in our family house. My mother will stand by you, I am sure. She will support you and the child. Take care of her in return. She has nobody else in this world. Please do not fall out with her. Let our child spend as much time with her grandmother as possible. And as for your own future, you're free to decide what path to follow, but don't forget that I sacrificed my life in order for you and our child to live in a free, just and secure country.

You will never receive another letter from me, my sweet angelic wife. Please sit in our little garden sometimes in the evening, and think of me. I shall have the image of your beautiful eyes with me to my dying moment.

Farewell, and don't ever forget that all was for FREEDOM, EQUALITY, DEMOCRACY, INDEPENDENCE.

Hold your head high: you are the wife of a fighter for justice. You are an honest Hellene whose husband has been murdered by traitors.

Please tell my story to our child and explain that all was for a better future.

I must finish now. I beg your forgiveness for what has happened. But there was no other way. If, during our lives together, I upset you, please don't bear a grudge. I was only foolish. To my last breath I shall love you. Give a big kiss to our child whom I shall never know.

Be strong as I am strong. Do not fret about me.

I love you.

Yours forever,

John

Right across the letter and with rough bold red handwriting the censor had written *WITH THE COMPLIMENTS OF THE PRISON SERVICES, AND KEEP THIS FOR THE REST OF YOUR LIFE TO REMEMBER WHAT A TRAITOR YOUR HUSBAND WAS.*

Zoë brought her lips up to the letter and kissed it. Her eyes couldn't hold her tears any longer. They ran down her delicate face. Her kiss on the letter was soft, gentle and careful, so the dampness from her face wouldn't damage the treasured words. She folded the letter carefully and placed it inside her pocket. Her thighs had been sweating under the silk skirt, because of the body heat of the cat. Her eyes wandered over to the little island two nautical miles away. 'He's there,' she thought to herself. 'He's buried with the others—but at least he has company. Is he at peace with his friends? Wouldn't it have been better if he'd stayed with us? Maria's now seven years old. Wouldn't he have liked to spend time with her? Wouldn't he have liked to grow old with me? My soul and his mother's have died with him. The world has gained nothing.'

She tried to remember her husband's face. She felt his presence but her memory couldn't recreate his face. She kept stroking the cat, which purred and licked her fingers. She stroked her again and again. She loved this cat. Her people had also abandoned her. She was also persecuted. Nobody could understand the cat's desperation. I wish I were a cat, or a bird–anything, so as to feel this heartache no longer, thought Zoë. Who could ever really understand her?

The more Zoë cuddled the cat, the more she purred in her lap. Zoë kept looking at the sea and the island. A boat reached the shore, and people started disembarking. Then they hurried home to wash and to get ready for the night's fiesta. Zoë watched another little boat travelling north. It was small and insignificant, just like the *Achilleas*.

She tried hard to focus on John's face. He had been blond and his eyes blue. He had a tan from the sun, since he was an amateur fisherman. His eyebrows had been the colour of straw, and followed a special line, but she couldn't now place them on the outline or shape of his face. His lips had been full, like juicy apricots, and when they kissed they had tasted sweet. She had kept saying to him: 'Kiss me. Kiss me on the mouth; you have the sweetest lips in the world.' He would laugh and his sharp white teeth would touch her tongue. Then she would break away and laugh too.

She couldn't remember life without him. They had been born in the same neighbourhood. Their mothers had been the best of friends, and took turns in looking after them. As children, they shared their toys and were always together. Zoë had photographs of them both standing next to their tricycles, holding hands in front of some bushes and smiling for the camera. Then they had gone to school together, and sat next to each other at the same desk.

In the classroom, John was the cleverest of them all. She wasn't so good, and since her mother needed her back home, she only stayed for four years, just long enough to learn to read and write. John continued studying. His best friend then was Anthony, who would later become a priest. But at some point, when such ideas started forming, Anthony followed the path of Christ while John insisted that there was no such thing as God, only injustice. Why was all the wealth in the hands of the church and the very few, when the rest of the people had so little?

'According to you, Anthony, the King and the church are like the heads of a big family, to which we all belong,' said John. 'If you were the head of the family and so rich, would you leave your children to starve? Go without clothes? Sleep five in a room because you were too mean to spend your money? Deprive them of education because you didn't want to contribute? Leave them to die because nobody would pay the doctor's bill? Would you accept all these miseries, when the heads of the family live a luxurious life, indulge in trivial hobbies to pass their idle time, and support charities that are merely reminders of the gulf between the haves and the have-nots? Is all that fair?'

Anthony would stare at him arrogantly and say: 'If you want it any different, go to Russia!' 'But I don't want to go to Russia,' John would reply. '*This* is my home. This is where I want to see things get better. I want to see all of us living decently, all our children fed, warmly clothed and well-educated, with proper medical attention from the time they're born until the day they die. I don't want some of us to have to worry about how we're going to bury our dead, how we're going to find a doctor, how we're going to provide even enough to feed the family.'

'Politics—all politics,' Anthony would say with a sardonic smile that drove John mad with anger. 'The King keeps us together,' was the best he could come up with. But on the existence of the church, he had a lot to say. He had been a church child all his life. His father had been a priest before him. Anthony saw God as the provider of everything. The church gave him security, order and made him what he was: a Hellene and an Orthodox man. The church was the best Hellenic institution, he thought, and it preserved the country's nationalist spirit. Anything other than belief was a betrayal.

After World War II, Anthony became a priest and John married Zoë. The couple lived on his mother's wealth. He talked intensely about ideas. Marx and the Soviet Union were his favourite topics. Anthony got married soon after, was ordained and placed himself inside the realm of the church. Not long afterwards he confessed to Zoë that he didn't love his wife. His heart was elsewhere.

Perhaps his heart had been given totally to the church, Zoë had innocently assumed. This of course would not necessarily stop him having many children as well as a mistress. It was common knowledge in Portovecchio. Perhaps Anthony's faith protected him. He was fortunate, the survivor.

Zoë believed in John's integrity and trusted what he told her—but he hadn't entrusted her with the whole truth about his activities. He had been a secret member of the Communist Party ever since becoming eligible to join. He believed in a thunderous Revolution for Hellas. Stalin had always been his role model. John could only see Hellas' future after World War II as a socialist state, a satellite of the Soviet Union. *Power to the Poor* was his credo.

From the age of eighteen John always claimed that he was looking for a job, but his mother's financial means conveniently removed the need for any sense of urgency. He carefully hid his activities as secretary of the local Communist Party. He told Zoë that he was busy organising the fledgling football club. Neither Zoë nor anybody else outside the members knew that the football club was really a socialist cell. From time to time the muscular footballers left for the mountains, and, after killing a few Nationalists, they returned as if nothing had happened. They wore their football club's shirts with pride.

John was not one of these. He was delicate and gentle, the party's bureaucrat, always writing and keeping notes. His weak constitution excluded him from action on the football pitch or anywhere else. The truth of the matter was that he was a good-for-nothing idle ideologue who would do anything for his beliefs.

Anthony knew nothing of all this. It was merely evil coincidence that he would be the one to betray John to the police as a Communist. Anthony's motive was vengeful jealousy. He loved Zoë. Little did he know that he was handing over to the authorities the most learned and solid socialist of Portovecchio.

Although John loved Zoë, he never owned up to her. She had to be kept out of all this, he felt. He considered her too fragile and dear to be involved. It was no wonder that she was shocked at the turn of events.

Now she lifted the cat in her arms and got up. She walked into the kitchen and deposited the animal carefully on a cushion on a chair by the open window. She washed her hands under the tap, and summoned the maid to the kitchen.

'Theodora, have you prepared the chicken for tomorrow?' she asked the maid, hiding and suppressing her emotions, as she always did at this time of year.

'Yes, of course,' said Theodora. 'Everything's ready. The chicken's been killed and I've jointed it. I put it on a platter covered with a tea towel. It's in the icebox.' Then she added impertinently: 'Don't forget it's my day off tomorrow. You'll have to do the cooking.'

She wanted to leave. 'Can I take Maria and go with her and her grandmother to see the procession now? It's nearly eight o'clock and everybody is already at the front. The bands have arrived, and the schoolchildren. Can't you hear them? If we don't get to the main road quickly, we'll never get a good place. I'm so short–I always end up behind somebody's back, and can't see.'

'Off you go then,' Zoë said, almost indifferently.

Theodora called little Maria, who came running out of her bedroom. They hurried to the front of the house to wait for the festival procession. Mamee the cat, as soon as she heard Theodora delivering her speech, jumped down from the chair and vanished like lightning.

The church bells had started ringing. Darkness had settled over Portovecchio, but hundreds of coloured lights illuminated the street. This was the night for gigantic *frigathelia*. Everywhere slaughtered lambs were being roasted on spits. The smell was heavenly. Louisa, Blossom and Tony were already standing outside their house, as were Renee and her mother Joy. Everyone was dressed in his or her best. They carried long white candles, lit as if by magic.

A whisper went through the crowd: 'They're coming. They're coming!' The procession was on its way up the hill.

Bands were playing and primary school children, summoned in the middle of their precious summer holidays, carried baskets of fresh flowers. Altar boys carried a canopy on their backs with a glorious icon of the Virgin Mary underneath it.

Suddenly the silence was broken by bursts of laughter. 'Look! Look who's there in front of Father Anthony!' Of course it was Mamee the cat. She was walking proudly, provocatively, slowly, a couple of yards in front of the procession, leading it. Father Anthony followed her, shaking a censer. Beneath his pious look, he was seething. He could hardly curse in public or kick the cat, since the distance between them was too great. He kept swinging the censer towards his parishioners on the right and left of the road. When he came to Zoë he bowed and directed his perfumed blessing towards her. She smiled at him and crossed herself. All the neighbours thought what a charitable priest he was.

Fat Foni, standing next to her husband, silently cursed Zoë. The special acknowledgment that she saw Anthony give her reminded Foni yet again where his heart really belonged. 'He still loves her,' she thought, and her memory brought back the time when he had screamed Zoë's name at the peak of their lovemaking. He had then threatened Foni viciously that if she opened her big mouth to anybody he would excommunicate her, and cut her stipend forever.

Everybody at the procession enjoyed seeing Mamee the cat in her new position. She didn't hesitate, or change her mind about leading the way. She guided the procession to the church, where she paused. Then, indifferently, calmly, and oblivious to all that was happening around her, she disappeared into the adjoining olive grove.

Did the Portovecchians really believe the priest's Christian generosity towards Zoë? Who can see into their thoughts? Paul, Fat Foni's husband, stood next to her, one arm short, bent double, facing the ground, seeing little of the procession. But he did see Mamee the cat marching, and laughed just like everyone else. When the icon of the Virgin Mary passed, he crossed himself three times. He believed that the Virgin had saved his life when the dynamite exploded. The loss of his arm had been a comparatively light punishment, and he had promised that he'd never use dynamite again and always do what Father Anthony, the Virgin Mary's agent on earth, told him to do. That was why he welcomed him warmly to his house. Perhaps losing his arm was a sign and a warning. Paul had become the most faithful member of Father Anthony's parish.

The evening of 14 August ended with the bands playing in the square, the lamb devoured, and gossip flourishing.

The following day everyone woke early. Some people went to church, others cooked and the lucky ones went to the beach. The children splashed and screamed in the sea. The heat was unbearable. Every year the celebration of the Assumption of the Virgin Mary was spent the same way in Portovecchio.

Since Theodora had the day off, Zoë started cooking lunch. She got the chicken out of the icebox. She washed it carefully, plucked it and, over a lit candle, burned off all the feathers that had been left by lazy Theodora. She cleaned it well and rubbed it with salt and plenty of black pepper. She placed it in a roasting tin. Then she peeled and quartered potatoes and placed them around the chicken, over which she sprinkled more salt and pepper. She squeezed two lemons and poured the juice over the chicken and the potatoes. She poured in plenty of olive oil and added a cup of warm water to the tin. She placed the two squeezed lemon halves inside the chicken's stomach, together with a peeled red onion, just for flavour. Then she added a large handful of oregano. She placed the baking tray in the preheated oven at 180 degrees.

She knew that Maria and John's mother would be delighted with this traditional, festive meal. While the chicken was roasting, she washed and sliced three big red tomatoes, one cucumber and a little white onion. She put them all in her best salad bowl and added crumbled feta and olives. Just before they were ready to eat she'd add olive oil and vinegar. They would accompany these dishes with bread and sliced *lefkaditiko* salami. Some Fix beer would be put on the table, just for fun, since none of the women drank anything apart from water.

For Zoë the salami was the best part of the meal. It was small, stout and dark red. Once sliced, the white fat stood out against the ruby red meat like rich spotted marble. She loved that salami, and it was served as a ritual at all their family's celebrations. Was there any better salami in the world?

Fat Foni stayed at home. She also cooked. She was annoyed at Father Anthony's attention towards Zoë the previous day. She secretly hoped that after the service the priest would drop by for a *triple sec* and a delicate cupcake she'd bought from the town's cake shop. It turned out that he didn't. Tired from the service and the procession the night before, he simply locked the church and went home. He was sweating profusely and in a really bad temper. The image of Zoë in her black silk dress, with her raven hair and her huge brown eyes, was driving him insane.

His wife had also roasted chicken, and the house was full of the fragrance of lemon and oregano. She was laying the table, scantily clad as usual. But seeing her body only turned his stomach. He ignored her. He went out into the garden and began to water in a manic manner. His wife, Helena, began cursing him. 'You idiot–you don't water the garden in such heat in the middle of the day! This is also a holy day, and a day of rest. Don't you know, *you* of all people, that this kind of labour is not allowed on a day like today?'

'Go to Hell!' he screamed at her, turning the hose on himself. Saturated, his black cassock, now wet and limp, stuck to his handsome body.

Lunch on 15 of August was a huge affair in all the homes in Portovecchio. A siesta followed. In the afternoon Zoë, Maria and her grandmother opened the shutters of their drawing room wide to receive their friends and neighbours. It was the only time of the year that they kept open house, to mark Maria's name day, her birthday and the anniversary of John's death.

Now Theodora came as a visitor, accompanied by her family. Renee arrived with her mother, and of course there were the newcomers, Tony, Blossom and Louisa. They were good neighbours, although Tony was always grumpy. Blossom had an uncertain smile on her face, and always walked a few steps behind the other two, like a wobbly duck. Tony habitually ignored her. He walked at the front, holding Louisa by the hand. She kept pulling it to break away from him.

Tony noticed Blossom only when she annoyed him. Then he snapped at her. Unless she had something important to say, Louisa never addressed either of them. It was pretty obvious to

Zoë that there wasn't much love there. It was said that Louisa's mother had died a few years back, and that he had never recovered. Information regarding everybody and their business spread with fantastic speed in Portovecchio. They all knew that Tony was a widower, a barrister, a man with *gravitas*, and someone whose superior education and intellect allowed him to be grumpy.

Tony had something of a reputation as a War hero, which added to the respect he was given. People looked up to his family, in contrast with Zoë's, who were marked as 'the Communist sympathisers'. Tony was also a published poet. Every week he had one of his verses published in the *Poets' Corner* of the *National Herald*. During the Wartime Italian Occupation, however, this talent had nearly got him into trouble with the Italian governor. He had written a long anti-Fascist poem, *To Kerkyra, Enslaved, 28 April 1941 to 28 April 1942*, in what was supposed to be Homeric style. In it he called Rome 'a whore', the Pope 'Antichrist', and so on:

Rome, the great prostitute, attacked you,
Rome's armed murderers and Fascists invaded;
They came in the dark, deceitfully, dishonestly,
And the Pope, the Antichrist, made the sign of the Cross!...

He had gone in the middle of the night and slipped it under the door of the governor's office. All Hell had broken loose. Tony was suspected as the culprit, since the style of the writing was more or less the same as his published verse. He was caught and imprisoned, and if it hadn't been for his barrister friends, who had secretly befriended the Italian

Fascists, he would have been executed. In any case, the Italians were much more lenient than the Germans and the Greek Communists, from whom one couldn't always escape alive.

After Tony was released, towards the end of the War, he had been travelling on a village bus when some British planes flew overhead. Based on faulty intelligence, they thought the bus was full of Germans. They fired on the bus, killing many innocent Greeks. Fortunately Tony survived, but was left with a lame leg for the rest of his life. His compatriots had showered him with respect since then. He had been wounded.

Louisa, his little girl, was sweet, people thought, if rather pale. She had the most extraordinary curly hair and sapphire blue eyes and was forever jumping and singing as if she had not a care in the world. She never mentioned her real mother. Everyone knew that she loved the cat which had become the furry mascot of Portovecchio.

Zoë liked this new family in spite of the fact that Blossom was uncouth and a peasant. She was, however, generous with her domestic advice and recipes. Having married so young, Zoë lacked experience in running a house, so was always eager to strike up a conversation in order to gain advice.

After everybody settled down in the elegant drawing room, Louisa pulled herself away from her father's side and, with the other girls, called the cat, who had settled comfortably again on Zoë's silky lap. They went into another room to play.

Father Anthony had arrived at Zoë's house accompanied by his wife and two of his children. Zoë offered them sour cherry juice, almond cakes and *nougatina*. You couldn't have the Assumption of the Virgin Mary without *nougatina*. This cake was never made at home. It was always bought at a certain cake shop in town. It was made with cream and pastry and thickly coated with chopped almonds. Towards the end of the visit, and as tradition had it, the adults were served *triple sec*, a sweet liqueur that everybody liked and expected.

As it was every year, the occasion at Zoë's house was quite sombre. No birthday cake was served. The guests never knew what greetings to give: 'Happy Birthday', 'Happy Name Day' or 'We're so sorry your husband was such a dreadful Communist and we're so glad he has gone for ever.' The adults talked and talked, avoiding any offensive topic.

Everyone was dressed in their finery. Father Anthony looked extremely handsome with his red hair, his hazel eyes and his black cassock. His wife looked at everyone sideways and kept reminding him that it was time to go, even though they had just arrived. The priest drank more *triple sec* than anybody else, and his cheeks were red and flushed, but he was excused, since it was such a special day.

Tony didn't like him at all and barely spoke a word to him. His relationship with religion since his wife's death was one of hate and resentment. Father Anthony kept asking him inappropriate questions about which cemetery she was buried in and where he wished to be buried himself. Wouldn't it be better if he moved the family grave from the town to Portovecchio? Tony declared that he had just paid a vast amount of money to purchase his family plot in town. Blossom smiled and lowered her gaze, since it was her money that had bought that bit of real estate.

At around seven o'clock they all left to get ready for the fiesta. In the evening the bands came back and everybody danced, while Mamee the cat looked on. Renee, Maria and

Louisa wore their new organdie dresses and Maria had a new golden chain hanging around her neck, this year's name day present from her grandmother. Louisa carried her doll in her arms and kept an eye on Mamee, hoping that she wouldn't be tempted to go searching in their kitchen while everyone was out celebrating. But the cat carried on walking around the bandstand and stretching herself. She had been born and bred here, so she really had as good a claim on her land as anybody else.

Theodora was the star of the evening. Somehow she must have saved money from the meagre wages she received from Maria's grandmother and spent it all on this year's outfit. She looked glamorous, youthful and beautiful. Her blonde hair had been tied up in a ponytail, and her starched petticoat pushed out her whole skirt around her slender thighs. She looked like a big but rather sexy parachute. She danced and danced and every time she swirled, everyone could see her white knickers.

Father Anthony's eyes bulged. In spite of the fact that his wife had told him to be home early that night after finishing his duty at the church, he had got rid of his ecclesiastical garments and changed back into his black cassock. Then he went to observe the bands playing and the young dancing. He was more than slightly tipsy, since he had been left with more Communion wine than usual. Someone handed him a brown bag with roughly-cut, still-warm pieces of lamb-on-the-spit and he devoured them with his fingers, poking the morsels into his mouth through his red curly beard. The August fast had left him hungry and bad-tempered.

When Theodora stopped dancing she approached him with a smile. She bent and kissed his greasy hand, out of respect. He stared at her blonde hair. Then she went to join Zoë, her mother-in-law and the girls. She was hot and breathless.

'Come and rest, child,' the old woman said. 'Enough for tonight. Don't you think you should go home now? There's a lot of work to be done tomorrow and I want you at our house by seven o'clock.'

'Yes, Signora,' the young girl responded, with hypocritical respect. She had her own plans to meet up with her young sailor lover at the cemetery, as arranged. The cemetery was behind the church, far away from all the festivities. Who would go there on such a special night? She helped herself to a bit more lamb from Anthony's bag, and then wishing them all 'Good Night', with a special 'Many Happy Returns' to Maria, she departed.

Father Anthony waited for a while. Then, carelessly throwing away his brown bag, he also left, after shaking hands with Zoë and her mother-in-law.

The moon was shining over Portovecchio. The smell of lamb penetrated every nook and cranny. The little square where the fiesta was taking place was lit by hundreds of multicoloured lights shining over the revellers. Away from the main road, however, everything was sunk deep in darkness, hidden by the night. Theodora knew her way well; she wandered behind the church and into the cemetery. She wasn't afraid. As a child, she had used it as a playground. She walked slowly, passing between the graves. There her old Grade One teacher was buried, and over there she could see her grandmother's photo glaring from a marble cross. She paused to stroke the cross lightly. Mamee the cat followed her.

Theodora was happy in anticipation of her sailor lover, and the cat's presence reassured her. Then suddenly somebody grabbed her and pulled her down. With urgent, rough movements a man lifted her short, frilly skirt and reached under the starched petticoat. He covered her mouth with his big hand. Theodora could smell incense, and wine on his breath. She didn't faint. She stared into his hazel eyes. She clenched her teeth; she grabbed at his cassock. Beside them was a colossal grave on top of which sat Mamee, staring down at them both.

The man moaned quietly, while threatening that one word out of her and she was dead, excommunicated, cursed.

Chapter 6

Morsels of octopus dipped in vinegar assist a fisherman's daughter

The Old Port, the slaughterhouse;
The sea runs red
Where children swim in blood.

September–October 1956

The square table in the small kitchen was covered with a plastic tablecloth. It was of a vibrant, multicoloured pattern with huge red juicy slices of watermelon splattered here and there. Orange and yellow were mixed gaily with blue and red. If one's taste in design inclined towards the absurd, this tablecloth deserved the prize. The green-and-white watermelon rinds had been exaggerated in thickness and colour.

Round this table a family had gathered for its midday meal. The kitchen had a big door so that their huge fishing baskets could be pushed in and out. This door was wide open and through it the garden and the sapphire-blue sea could be viewed.

In Portovecchio certain things could be enjoyed without any outlay of money. Ordinary pleasures, which in other parts of the world would cost a fortune, were freely available to all. There was throughout the year a light both intense and dazzling, a pink light that sparkled on the blue sea. It bounced off the silver-green leaves of the olive trees, off the rose bushes, off the whitewash of the houses. Even when the clouds were heavy, loaded with rain and hanging low, Portovecchio could be seen through a magical filter, neither pink nor bright but platinum, consisting of all shades of pearly grey and confirming the fact that Nature is mightier than all the artists in the universe.

The humidity, the heat, the cold, the rain and the wind of the Ionian Sea never undermined this wonderful light. They only modified it. For most of the three hundred and sixty-five days of the year the daylight was bright and the sky a spotless blue. This gift of the gods extended to the night-time, too, when billions of stars lit the boundless sky. When there was a full moon a brilliant light spread over the sea and the island. Gods and demigods could be expected to climb down from the heavens and dance. The galaxy was clearly visible. Even the youngest children could identify the Milky Way, the Big and Small Bears, Venus and Hermes.

Every year the Portovecchians continue to be amused by the hordes of Northern Europeans who pay a small fortune to come and enjoy what they themselves have for free and in abundance. This makes them a touch smug and arrogant. They laugh at the way the foreigners unwrap and expose their usually heavily clothed bodies to the sun. The Hellenic sun, almost out of spite, invariably burns and blisters flabby white flesh. The foreigners have paid dearly for the privilege. They hope to buy the sun, a share of a dream. But the sun, a stranger to them, only torments them.

In old Portovecchio, almost all dwellings had a grand view of the sea. This made no difference to the price of real estate. These were just houses for people to live in, not used to impress each other. The mountains across on the mainland, whether snow-capped or tinted pink by the sunset, always appeared awe-inspiring. Every so often the Portovecchians' religious superstition reminded them that they ought to be grateful for what God has given them. They would stop what they were doing and look around, take a deep breath and observe the beauty of their environment, comment on it, cross themselves, then bend their bodies again in order to carry on doing their work.

The beauty of the land and sea were not the only priceless resources they enjoyed. Commercially-produced perfume sprays were also an unnecessary luxury. The most delicate perfumes were provided by rose petals, orange and lemon blossom, honeysuckle, hydrangeas, lilies, freesias, marigolds, gardenias, jasmine, bougainvillea, mulberries, fig trees and prickly pears, which grew everywhere in abundance. Everyone had a selection of these plants in their garden. No expert advice was needed to make anything grow. You just planted anything you wanted.

Landscape gardeners were also unknown, and no-one bothered to mention the fruit. It was just there, tasty, free and in abundance. This was the wealth of the owners of the kitchen with the colourful plastic tablecloth.

The kitchen was whitewashed, bright and very clean, although poor in terms of equipment and furniture. The sea breeze kept it cool, shady and comfortable. Its flagstones had been washed that September morning and gave off a shiny, refreshing sparkle. On the table there was a wooden board with fresh brown bread, a bottle of olive oil, two juicy yellow lemon-halves, and a platter with a huge boiled lobster surrounded by numerous pink prawns. Inexpensive cutlery and crockery had been put haphazardly on the table. Plain, well-polished water glasses of various sizes surrounded a clay jug of water. There was also a bowl full of *orzo*, pasta the size of grains of rice. It was bright red in its tomato sauce and steaming, just off the stove. The family was ready to start eating.

A large poster of an angel resting his round Baroque face on his palms had been stuck up on one of the walls above the dining table. This cherub was dressed in a white robe and had large white wings protruding from his back. He had bright red curly hair, and looked serene and wise. He seemed to recognise this family's goodness, and the love among its members. They crossed themselves and, after whispering a prayer of thanksgiving, tucked into the food.

It had cost them very little. Father and son, the fishermen, had caught the prawns and lobster themselves. The mother, Adelaide, had picked the lemon from her own tree, and bought the *orzo* for a minimal sum. The cost of olive oil in those days was negligible.

That morning, before she knew what the men would catch, Adelaide had boiled water in a saucepan with salt, and when it came to the boil, added about 250 grams of *orzo*. In the meantime she had picked tomatoes from their garden, mashed them with her hands and put them through the colander. She added this tomato purée, with the addition of some tomato paste and a teaspoon of sugar, to the *orzo*. She stirred, and then she added olive oil on top. After eight to ten minutes the *orzo* was ready: warm, bright red, each grain separate and cooked just a degree above *al dente*. She served it in a big bowl beside the lobster and the prawns.

Adelaide was always telling her family that you should never do anything to prawns and lobster except boil them in salted water. She also told them never to put anything else on them apart from lemon juice and olive oil. Let the foolish people of the world pay fortunes for shellfish cooked in fancy ways. Making lobster and prawns suffer under the burden of intricate and over-dominating sauces was a sin, she believed. Let the lobster and the prawns remain natural and free so the taste buds can jump for joy!

Undemanding, hard-working, sun-bleached and loving, there they were: the mother, the father, George, their son Peter, and their elder daughter Theodora. Away in the corner nearest the garden door, the youngest child, Alice, was resting in her special deck chair. She was too exhausted from her disease to sit up and take a meal at the table with the others.

Adelaide had been born in Adelaide, South Australia, to poor immigrant parents. Their emigration from Kerkyra to Australia had proved a failure, and after their daughter was born they decided to return to Portovecchio. They called the girl Adelaide in order to commemorate their only trip outside their small and insignificant island. She was a reminder for the rest of their lives of some connection with that faraway land. They never regretted returning. They remained poor, but their experience convinced them that it is better to be poor in a small fishing suburb on Kerkyra than in a city of the industrialised world with its ruthless free market.

Adelaide's father's skills in fishing enabled him to feed his family, and when she grew into a pretty young woman, they married her off to George, her father's fishing partner and distant cousin. Although the marriage was by arrangement, they grew to love each other passionately and with deep mutual respect. They produced three children, but never enough income to relieve their anxieties about their poverty.

Their first child was Theodora, meaning gift from God. When she was ten years old she was sent to work as a maid at the big house up the road belonging to an elderly woman called Emilia. She had a Communist son who had been executed—or at least that's what people said. Emilia, who lived with her daughter-in-law Zoë and grand-daughter Maria, took good care of Theodora. As long as she performed her cleaning duties responsibly, everyone was happy and kind to her. Emilia's family, with its tragic political background, was good and generous, and although Theodora collapsed on her mattress on the floor from fatigue every night, she knew they loved her. They also rewarded her generously. In their treatment of Theodora, they remembered and honoured the executed Communist son and husband, who always fought for the workers.

Emilia was a Cerberus over housework matters. She was tidy, clean and house-proud beyond belief. Her demands on Theodora were many and heavy, but she fed the girl three meals every day and bought her anything that was necessary, such as clothes and shoes. This was a great help to George and his family.

After Theodora, Peter was born. He was without doubt the best-looking boy in Portovecchio. At sixteen, he was tall, blond and blue-eyed. The constant exposure to the sun and the sea had turned his body a golden honey colour. His muscles were tight and his casual, carefree walk filled the girls with yearning. He went fishing with his father, he cleaned and mended the boat, and in his free time he played with his younger sister Alice, Adelaide and George's third child. Father and son, both as blond as gold, presented a strong contrast, the young boy an Apollo, the father thin and leathery like all the fishermen in Portovecchio once they passed the prime of their youth. But the smile in George's blue eyes, still there after so many years of hard work, made Adelaide the happiest woman in the district.

At least she would have been the happiest woman in Portovecchio, were it not for the heavy burden the family had to bear because of their youngest child's disease. Their non-existent wealth never bothered them. They lived contentedly in their tiny house. Their garden was full of fishing-nets and fruit trees. They never envied other families who lived just a little further up and who seemed to have everything. They all ate well and had plenty to do. Their cross, however, was Alice's incurable disease.

The family owned a precious little fishing boat, which they had named after Alice. It was moored only a few yards away from the bottom of their garden. The name was painted in brilliant blue on the white wood.

Father and son always seemed boisterous, full of fun and energy. The Portovecchians relied on them to provide good fish. To the neighbours, they seemed stoic, brave, as if taking everything in their stride. But beneath the surface they were filled with sadness and anxiety about Alice's condition. This anxiety was eating them up.

Adelaide was small and quiet, with hair the colour of smooth, shiny chestnuts. Her back was a little bent from years of hard work, but her love for her family was limitless. Her pain, on account of Alice, was everlasting.

Alice was eleven. Sometimes she appeared like a vulnerable baby, and at others she resembled a woman advanced in years. She wasn't the colour of gold and honey like her siblings. She was a sickly yellow colour. Her stomach, in comparison to the rest of her body, was enlarged, so she had the shape of a pregnant dwarf woman. Her eyes were pale blue but surrounded by dark circles. She walked slowly and looked timidly at the world. She wore a half-smile on her face, an imprint of selfless kindness.

Alice harboured no resentment at her condition. She was too young to consider the reality of a healthy world outside herself. She would have loved to be out and about, playing with the other children, swimming and sunbathing without having to be carried everywhere by either George or Peter. But it never crossed her young mind to be bitter. Sometimes her condition, when she was not in pain, even gave her a kind of pleasure. She was accustomed to being the centre of attention and love. She loved to feel the warmth of her brother's and father's bodies close to her. She always tried to be friends with the children in the neighbourhood and included in their games. Sadly, most of them couldn't be bothered with her because she couldn't easily move around. Only Louisa, Renee and Maria, who were a little younger than she was, provided regular amusement for Alice, partly because she was related to Peter and Theodora. They possessed lots of fascinating toys, toys that their better-off parents could afford to buy. They let her play with their dolls, and their dolls' possessions. Alice loved that but shrank back when their games involved boisterous movement. Unfortunately she could never keep up with them and their adventures from her deck chair when they were out and about. She couldn't run at all and when she walked she had to rest every so often. When she was younger she had been more active, but as the years progressed she slowed down, as the disease intensified.

In Portovecchio the sight of Alice being carried by George or Peter had become familiar to everyone. The two men walked erect, blond, tanned, in their turned-up shirtsleeves and trousers, with no shoes. They carried their precious load on their shoulders and they always had huge smiles on their faces. They felt the same pride as when, at other times, they carried on their heads their baskets full of fish for sale. The Portovecchians always greeted them with friendly enthusiasm. Alice, her family and the fish were part of their lives.

Alice looked like a queen up there on their shoulders, a pale queen from an age-yellowed magazine. She wore dainty clothes with lots of lace, when other children were in shorts, or little skirts. Her father spoiled her by walking her around and talking to her, taking her everywhere he went. His wife, frail and tired as she was, never went out with Alice. She took care of her indoors. Theodora bought her small inexpensive toys.

After she had finished her housework and tended her little garden, which was covered with a shady, grape-laden vine, Adelaide cleaned the fish in an outside basin, or put the washing out to dry. Then she would sit next to Alice, reclining on her deck-chair under the almond tree, and tell her stories about faraway Australia, the kangaroos and the possums. She hardly remembered her Australian existence, but after they came back from Adelaide, her parents never stopped talking about that extraordinary continent. So the oral history of their lives in South Australia was transferred to Portovecchio, told time and time again and exaggerated.

Adelaide had a very gentle way of talking. Most Portovecchians were aggressive, loud and very matter-of-fact. There were not many niceties in the way they communicated. Living without frills doesn't require fancy language. But Adelaide was always softly-spoken and used terms such as *dear*, *darling*, *sweetie*, *love* and *my favourite girl*. She was generous with her *thank you's* and *please's*.

Alice loved lying in her deck chair watching and listening to her mother. On Mondays, when the washing was hanging out, she would sit on her deck chair for hours with Mamee the cat on her lap. She would stroke the cat with her bony hands, and make up songs to sing to her. Every so often she would raise her little head to watch the movement of the brilliant white washing drying in the sea breeze. In the evenings, the deck chair would be brought into the front garden facing the road. George would put Alice there, covered with her rug, and mother and daughter would take part in the evening rituals of Portovecchio. Adelaide would knit new fishing nets. Alice, with the cat still on her lap, would listen to the gossip and wait patiently for the trio of wealthy girls to arrive and spend time with her.

Adelaide and Alice listened to any gossip, but never contributed to it. Their minds were too preoccupied with their own plight. They had no time to worry about the problems of the world. Sometimes when she was feeling weak, Alice would sit on her mother's lap with her head buried in her bosom. Then the cat would jump off her lap and curl up at Adelaide's feet.

Alice loved all her family, but she worshipped her brother Peter. He was so much taller than she was, so blond and strong. He was also a brilliant swimmer. Even if Alice had the strength to swim, she would not have been allowed to try. She merely paddled when the weather was scorching hot.

Peter walked with a swagger in his rolled-up trousers. Sometimes he wore a white shirt, sleeves pushed back to the elbows; sometimes he went bare-chested. By August every year his hair would be bleached white by the sun, but that only enhanced his beauty. He was so popular with the girls that they all wanted to rest their towels on his boat so they could have a chance to talk with him while he was sorting out the nets. In the evenings, they paraded in front of his house where he sat in silence, either playing with Alice or just keeping his mother company.

If Alice adored him, he loved her in return. She was so weak, so fragile. But her abdomen seemed to be swelling by the day. The neighbours gossiped. It was her spleen, they murmured. Nobody had a name for her disease, but it was common knowledge that she wouldn't live to grow old. She would die quite soon. The illness would kill her.

As the family sat round the table eating their delicious meal, Adelaide noticed that Theodora was not herself. Since the fiesta of 15 August she had been moody and snappy. Adelaide had caught her crying a few times. One day, no matter how much Adelaide called her, she refused to get out of bed and go to work. Adelaide had told George, and they both agreed that she must have some love trouble with her handsome sailor. Peter had been in a similar black mood when the midwife's family had left, taking their daughter, Peter's girlfriend, with them.

Adelaide knew that Theodora was supposed to have met up with her sailor on 15 August, but something must have happened, because she had come home after the fiesta with her face ashen white, a blank look in her eyes, and had gone to bed without uttering a word. Since then, in spite of the fact that she was trying hard to hide what was going on inside her, her mother could tell that something was not right. But poor Adelaide had enough to think about with Alice, without having to worry about Theodora's love life.

As they ate, someone commented every so often on the quality of the prawns and the lobster. George declared with pride that when he and Peter caught shellfish they would under no circumstances sell it to anyone else. The family came first. Their lives wouldn't alter much in any case as a result of the money they could bring.

When the meal was finished, Peter got up and pulled up a chair near Alice. She had only eaten the *orzo*, as shellfish made her sick. 'Hey little Alice, what's up?' he said laughingly, trying to tickle her. She protected herself by trying to push him away with her thin, outstretched hands.

'I'm not feeling all that good today,' she whined and laughed at the same time.

'Oh, no? What's wrong? You imagine things, silly girl. You want us to tell you all the time how much we love you and how much we dislike silly Theodora. Isn't that so, Mum?'

He turned to his mother, who didn't seem to know where to look first, towards tearful Theodora or pale yellow Alice. At that moment Mamee the cat walked elegantly into the kitchen. Ignoring the food, she jumped on to Alice's lap. Alice welcomed her gratefully.

'Oh, my darling sweet Mamee, give me a little kiss,' she said, and bent her big, almost deformed face to kiss the cat's own face.

Peter got up. 'You lucky thing–here's your best friend. You don't need me any more. I can go and tidy up my nets now, can't I?' he said, stroking the cat gently. Then he kissed Alice on her forehead.

Alice was so preoccupied with the cat that she scarcely noticed Peter going out to the garden to start taking care of his nets. Alice loved the cat so much. She was happy that her owners had gone and left her behind so she could have Mamee all to herself. She knew that she had other friends in the neighbourhood, but Alice believed she was her first and best friend. Some terrible people didn't like Mamee and even kicked her and sent her away, but most of the people in the neighbourhood gave her food so she wouldn't steal. Mamee never went to Alice for food, just for precious cuddles and warmth.

The meal over, George went to lie down. He and Peter had been up fishing since three o'clock that morning. Adelaide started clearing the table. Theodora declared that she had better go to work, since that morning she had not managed to get out of bed before midday and even then only after Adelaide had pleaded with her several times.

'Theodora, you're so lazy these days,' said her mother. 'What's going on?'

'Nothing, Mother. I keep telling you.'

'Where's your sweet sailor?'

'I have no idea. I think he's going to be sent to a ship. He'll be leaving soon.'

'Is that why you're so sulky?'

'Yes, Mother,' said Theodora, very calmly. Any answer would do to stop Adelaide asking questions. Theodora was tired and feeling sick. Her period was late and after that nightmare at the cemetery, her body didn't seem to function properly. But what could she say to her mother? Alice provided worries enough for all of them, after all.

'I'm off now,' said Theodora as she made for the door, leaving Adelaide still wondering what was really wrong.

On the way to work Theodora felt nauseous. She rushed off the path behind an oleander bush on the side of the road and started vomiting. One possible explanation for her condition frightened her to death. The first and lesser of two possible evils was that perhaps she had the same disease as Alice. The second possibility was that the disgusting encounter with Father Anthony had left her not only bruised but *with child*.

'Fancy carrying the child of the Devil inside me,' she thought with horror. 'What am I going to do? My parents, my boyfriend, the whole neighbourhood will find out! My life will be ruined. What shall I do with a baby?' She looked towards the church of the Virgin Mary and, clasping her hands underneath her apron and trying to look as normal as possible, she prayed hard that it might be the first of the two possibilities. Being sick was better than being covered with shame. Then she steadied herself and proceeded to Emilia's house in the full knowledge that she would receive a barrage of complaints from her employer.

Adelaide carried on talking to Alice in her soft, loving voice. Her daughter's responses were short and soft, almost a whisper. Eventually she fell asleep, exhausted, with Mamee still on her lap. Adelaide finished washing the dishes, and put an unnecessary blanket over Alice and the cat. The cat didn't like the cover. She jumped off and ran through the door into the garden.

Alice's sleep was heavy, and accompanied by a slight murmur, like a snore, a sound which, coming from her round little yellow mouth, seemed frightening and ominous. Adelaide took a good look at her and shook her head. Then she bent and kissed her cheek. She shut the door to the garden to keep the light out and lay on the small sofa they kept in the kitchen, to rest her weary body.

Everyone was taking a siesta, but Adelaide couldn't sleep. God had given her two beautiful strong children first, and then Alice. 'How long is my little baby going to live?' she thought. Since her birth she'd been so yellow, so sick. One doctor had said it was her spleen and another that it was her liver. Both had declared that she wouldn't live beyond the age of ten. She was eleven now. Could miracles happen?

Adelaide loved and cherished her daughter, but she also excluded her from her dreams of the future. She had resigned herself to the doctors' verdict. She knew that this little being wouldn't be with them for very long. Theodora and Peter were the only ones who were part of the bigger picture. They had enough to eat and sufficient to live their daily lives, sweet and peaceful near the sea in Portovecchio. Adelaide didn't even know whether Alice could have been saved if they had a lot of money and could have afforded the best medical care. She accepted it all with the fatalism that only brave, wise people possess.

Alice's father George did his best to make money from fishing and selling his catch. He was very clever at catching octopus and always had a good supply. He sold it in the restaurants in town, usually after keeping back a few of average size: about two kilos. He washed them and tenderised them by beating them against a rock by the sea. Then he put them into a huge saucepan of salted water. He boiled them until they were soft and a fork could easily pierce them. He drained them, let them cool and then chopped the tentacles up into cubes. He placed them in a rectangular baking tin, and poured a glass of very good red wine vinegar into a little dish in the corner of the tin. Everyone who wanted a bite would pick up a piece with a toothpick, dip it in the vinegar and eat it, after giving the fisherman the equivalent of ten pence.

George needed that money badly, for Alice's medical expenses. He was the kind of man for whom the value of money had to be visible, tangible, solid, not just numbers in a savings account in a bank. So when he got some money from the sale of fish or octopus, he would take it home and wrap the notes in a roll, securing them with a rubber band and placing them in the drawer of his bedside table. The thicker the roll, the stronger his confidence; the thinner the roll, the poorer his hopes, as Alice suffered and he became more depressed.

Friends would often ask him for his octopus recipe, but he never gave it to anybody. He was the only one in the neighbourhood who carried such a delicacy round the suburb every evening. He gave such pleasure to everybody.

October and Autumn arrived in their usual manner, with rain, wind, and thunder. The heat had subsided a few weeks before. The days were shorter now and the nights much cooler. The siestas had stopped, and Portovecchio was gradually getting ready to embrace the Winter. Autumn in Kerkyra isn't just wet, it's *very* wet, and every year the inhabitants forget what it was like the year before. They discuss how unusual each year's rainfalls are, forgetting that the same thing happens every year and that the same conversation also takes place.

The schools had been open since mid-September, and now were preparing for the celebrations of 28 October. The War was still fresh in the memory of the adults. The schoolteachers had been given the responsibility of rousing the consciences of the young by passing on their memories. The cruelty of one European nation towards the others must never be forgotten. They also had to remind themselves that this had occurred many times before. Nobody ever seemed to learn from the disasters. Could commemorations put an end to violence and safeguard the future? Of course not–but for Hellenes, the celebrations of 28 October, with their upsurge of national enthusiasm, were in fact a commemoration of how a small nation called Hellas had said a strong and determined '*NO*' to the aggressive Italians. On 28 October all Hellenes celebrated their nation's bravery and their resolve never to be occupied again. Children learnt to recite by heart poems written by national poets on the subject of '*NO*'. Laurel wreaths were hung above the portraits of national heroes; blue-and-white national flags were brought out of cupboards. Smart blazers were sent to the dry cleaners to get them ready for the big parade.

Louisa, Maria and Renee were excluded from everything because they were too young. There was one exception: because of Tony's famous 'Occupation epic', that had nearly cost the life of so many at the time, Louisa had to recite it in front of her school. Every year on the eve of 28 October she would dread having to stand on a podium and call Rome 'a whore' and the Pope 'the Antichrist'. But the whole school, teachers and pupils alike, loved it. The teachers loved it for its powerful content, and the children for the rude words.

Maria and Renee were disappointed that Louisa was being sent to school near her old home. Her father didn't want her to attend the Portovecchio school, which he considered educationally inferior, due to its high proportion of fishermen's children. Tony was a snob. He didn't want Louisa to mix with children like this. His snobbery was not, of course, greater than his need for money. If he'd had his own money, he would never have married Blossom. His snobbery and his hypocrisy served him for nothing, and yet he was full of both. He had convinced himself that his marriage to Blossom was for Louisa's good. But once a mother is lost, nobody can replace her. That's a fact, and anybody who says differently is fooling themselves. In spite of Louisa being so young, she could see that Blossom was intended to fill the place of Tina the maid and lighten the burden on Tony's pocket rather than fulfil her own childish emotional needs.

Tony was in fact correct in his decision to avoid a change of school for Louisa, if for the wrong reasons. He calculated that another drastic change in her life would not be a good idea. Every morning he put her on a small saddle he had added to the front bar of his bike and off they went together into town, leaving Blossom to do the chores. On the way Louisa waved and laughed to all the other children who were walking to their own school.

Her bike ride every morning was the best thing in her life. No more walking to school on her own with all the others

Morsels of octopus dipped in vinegar...

staring at her in pity. Now it was the others who must have been a little jealous of her new style of transport. The wind, blowing her wild hair away from her face, made her gasp for breath. Her blue eyes sparkled with happiness as she tightly grasped the handle-bars. Every so often she reached for the bell and rang it as they passed acquaintances, to attract their attention. Then she waved with pride and joy.

Blossom, left behind on her own, was also happy. Until lunchtime she would be queen in this lovely house. No reprimands, no sulking, no conformity to bourgeois living. She could wobble as much as she liked and eat as much as she liked, the way she liked. She could sit on the doorstep, legs apart, with her dirty apron on. She could gobble down brown bread soaked in olive oil accompanied by a big white raw onion.

When she had finished her housework, something she hated doing and never completed as well as the locals, she would take her distaff and work with lambs' wool for a couple of hours, to create a thick rough creamy white yarn that in the winter she would knit into socks for Tony. He invariably refused to wear them.

Swimming was not for her, especially in this blood-coloured sea. As for gardening, she would rather fill the place with tomatoes, cucumbers, lettuces and hundreds of onion and garlic plants. She didn't care for the dainty flowers that Tony had started planting. She would also have loved to fill the garden with chickens, and if she could have had a goat, so much the better.

She loved their new house, with its views and space outdoors. It gave her the limited freedom she needed. She was so accustomed to living outside the home in her village that she had found the apartment in town suffocating and restricting. Now she could come out of her kitchen as in her pre-marriage days and sit on the steps, eat there, knit there and sometimes just bask lazily in the sunshine, doing nothing. She wasn't destined to make friends with the local women, since she looked down on them, especially when they were working on their fishing nets. They, in turn, disliked her for her appearance and her way of speaking, all the roughness and ugliness about her. They thought she was stupid with her determination to spin wool. Who would wear such rough pullovers or socks these days? they wondered.

Blossom had been informed of the local women's amorous escapades, and detested them. She resented their freedom and their joy in sex. The local women were carefully groomed. If their clothes were not particularly expensive, they still had a provocative elegance about them that caused trouble among men. Blossom hated the words *morozo* or *moroza* that they frequently used in their local idiom. In her view the words were coarse, referring as they did to individuals involved in extra-marital affairs. Blossom imagined that every Portovecchian had been a *morozo* or *moroza* at some time in their lives. They were sensual and sexual. She wasn't interested in all that. Sex, smart clothes, elegant talk and refinements were not for her.

After he married Blossom, Tony never took her out with him or introduced her to his friends. He just left her in Portovecchio. It never crossed her mind that this was unnatural for a married couple. Her peasant upbringing had taught her to be so subservient and pathetically undemanding that in many ways she brought an extra dimension of misery into the household.

Louisa, who was young and had other things on her mind, never felt sorry for Blossom. Resentment was so paramount in her childish heart that it blocked out any consideration for this woman. But Louisa, in contrast with Blossom and Tony, slowly started liking the locals. She found them fascinating. They sparked her imagination. She had almost reached the point of forgetting her previous life in the old neighbourhood. The only link with the past, at the core of her existence, was her mother's death. This would never leave her and until the day she died she would sense a female presence always at her side. She could feel her mother's touch, smell her scent. This gave her comfort.

Portovecchio eventually paved her way to adulthood. With its colourful people, its dramas, the bloody sea and the squealing pigs, with the blond *morozas* and demigods, it became a wonderful source of fulfilment for young Louisa. Later she came to believe that God never completely abandons His own people.

She also took to swimming and life by the sea like a duck to water. She found a way to persuade Tony and Blossom to let her swim with her new friends when the slaughterhouse was not in operation. The aquamarine sea became part of her and her psyche. Her two intimate companions were the presence of her absent mother and the ever-present image of the sea. These two elements remained as Portovecchio contributed to the creation of a new, tough and self-sufficient Louisa.

On hot days nothing gave her greater pleasure than to go down to the beach with all the other children. In an innocent and immature display of coquetry, she and the other little girls would leave their towels on the *Alice* as it floated like a walnut shell on the water. And like the other girls, they hoped that Peter would offer them his salty smile.

Louisa was astonished at the way the sea replenished itself. Of course the water was never as clear as at other beaches, but it became clean enough, blue and refreshing.

When 28 October arrived, it was celebrated with a thanksgiving service and a big parade through the town, with all the important people laying wreaths at the Tomb of the Unknown Soldier. Everyone attended, young and old. The old were stern-faced, lost in their sad memories; the young were joyful since there was no school and the brass bands were playing thunderous and joyous tunes.

Chapter 7

The cat steals, eats and sleeps well, while Joy cooks an inedible *pastitsada*

*Fat Foni's fun to fondle,
But others pay the price.*

October–December 1956

Exhausted from all the excitement and loaded with blue-and-white balloons and flags, Louisa, Renee, Maria and Zoë took the bus back to Portovecchio from town.

It was lunchtime. People were either having their meal or were on their way home after a morning's labour. The neighbourhood appeared calm and quiet, but the sound of church bells could be heard, melancholy and faint. The bells of the church of the Virgin Mary were not ringing with joy as they had done on the morning of the national celebrations. Instead, they rang monotonously, one at a time, like the Good Friday tolling that announces the death of Christ. But it wasn't Spring and it wasn't Good Friday. What had happened?

As the four of them walked up the hill, their neighbours were coming out of their houses and standing in their front gardens, asking each other with intense curiosity why the bells tolled so mournfully.

'Alice is dead,' somebody said. The news spread fast throughout the neighbourhood. Nobody was surprised; it had been expected, after all.

Zoë, Maria and Renee covered their mouths with their hands. Their faces were transformed, like their neighbours', into masks of grief. Louisa, who had only known Alice for a short time, found that she felt nothing. What was the fuss about? They knew that this was inevitable, didn't they? Alice's death didn't move anything in her heart. Death had wounded her once, sharply, leaving no space for grief for others.

But curiosity suddenly overcame her. She thought of the bloated abdomen and the yellow face; then she thought of Alice's parents.

'The funeral will be tomorrow afternoon,' someone shouted.

'We'll all go,' Renee said. 'We'll go after school together and take her some flowers.' As they passed Alice's family's cottage, the shutters were tightly closed.

The next day, when Louisa returned home for lunch on the front bar of her father's bike, Renee and Maria were already waiting for her.

'Louisa, come on—get some flowers. We're going to see Alice,' they cried, full of excitement.

Louisa's curiosity had increased by many degrees. She thought to herself: 'Alice is dead, like my mother. What can she be like? The coffin, with my mum in it, I never saw. She's gone and I have no idea how she went. What kind of face did she have when she died? Are people different when they're dead? Do they still have flesh on them? Or does everything disappear and is only a skeleton left lying in the coffin?'

She knew she had to see Alice. She had to find out what had happened to her yellow-green face, her bloated tummy, her pale eyes, her blonde hair.

Louisa rushed into the house, gave her face a quick wash and got rid of her school uniform. She put on her blue pleated skirt, which was worn for special days at school. She dug a simple white pullover out of her drawer. Although now very tight on her, it completed what she considered appropriate attire.

Blossom handed her a bunch of flowers collected from their back garden. Some were white, others a deep yellow. Louisa didn't care very much about the flowers. They were chrysanthemums, with a very heavy scent. She ran out and joined her two friends. Together they climbed the hill to the little white church.

The view from up there was stunning. You could see the giant mountains of enemy Albania across the water. The little islands floating in the sea were oblivious to the tragedy. The sea that particular afternoon was as blue as it could be. The anchored fishing boats rocked slightly. It was the slaughter-house's day off. The sky was also a clear blue.

You could hear the swallows singing and watch them fly at speed from one electricity pole to another. It was cool and fresh after a storm the night before.

Louisa breathed deeply, took Renee's hand in her own and, holding her flowers tight, entered the church.

It had been built in 1543, according to the inscription above the door. The only improvement or addition since that time was the whitewashing of the outside walls, done twice a year. The local women carried out the job faithfully and carefully. They paid special attention to the belfry, which could be seen from miles away and also from the sea.

The church housed a precious icon of the Virgin Mary. It was in the style of the Cretan School. People were standing outside the church, smoking and chatting. The girls passed through the little crowd, brushing away the tobacco smoke. Slowly and timidly, they entered, blinking.

The interior seemed dark after the bright daylight. Many candles had been lit, as well as the central crystal chandelier. The silver ornaments of the church reflected the light of a thousand candles. In the middle there was a small white coffin with gilded decorations, covered in white chrysanthemums. Next to it were four chairs, and on them sat Peter and his father and mother, with Theodora. George had his best suit on, while Adelaide and Theodora were dressed in black, with black scarves around their heads and tied under their chins. Peter was dressed all in white, with a black band around his arm. His blond hair was a shade darker now that summer had faded. He looked younger than usual, and vulnerable.

Adelaide looked as if she were on another planet. George couldn't drag his eyes away from Alice's little face protruding ever so slightly from the coffin. Theodora looked pale and plump.

The girls approached, Renee first, then Maria, with Louisa following. They left their flowers at the foot of the open coffin. Poor Alice! You could see only her face and a little of her neck and tiny chest. She was dressed like a bride with a crown of lemon blossom around her well-combed hair. She was yellow no more, just white. Her eyes were half-closed and she wore an expression full of calm sweetness.

Everyone kissed her forehead, so Louisa had to do the same. Her lips touched the unexpectedly cold skin. It felt as if they were touching a piece of marble. There was silence in the church except for George's sobbing. Adelaide's face was cold and distant. She looked worn-out, bent, bony, drained. Theodora just looked ill. They were constantly wiping their tears. George and Peter looked stunned, as if some thunderous blow had bruised their faces. The whole family looked incomplete and lost.

'Alice will join the angels,' Blossom whispered from behind Louisa. She had followed the girls to the church at a distance, so they hadn't noticed her. Blossom didn't want Louisa to be there on her own. After they had kissed Alice, Blossom took Louisa's hand and pulled her gently towards her. Then they walked towards the grieving family and shook hands with them. They went outside to wait for the burial to take place.

The little coffin, now closed, was carried on the shoulders of four family friends towards the cemetery behind the church. Father Anthony followed it and behind him came a couple of boys from the neighbourhood, walking slowly and carrying flowers and wreaths.

Father Anthony looked grumpy and kept glancing sideways. The funeral procession approached the place where Alice was going to be buried. There, on a pile of freshly-dug soil sat Mamee, washing her face with one paw and turned towards the sun.

Father Anthony strode towards her and said in his usual vicious, whispering manner: 'Go to Hell, monster!' The cat didn't move. She stopped washing her face and turned her head towards the mourners.

Suddenly Theodora let out a scream and collapsed. Peter tried to lift her up. Her mother told her in a severe voice to pull herself together. Then she called Mamee in a gentle voice and beckoned her. The cat approached and Adelaide lifted her in her arms and stroked her. She told the grave-diggers to continue with the burial.

Soon it was all over. Everyone started walking back towards their houses. Adelaide held the cat gently in her arms all the way home.

Louisa's curiosity had been satisfied, although she remained unsure about the state of her mother's non-existence. How and where had she gone? Where was her disease-ravaged body buried?

Louisa let go of Blossom's hand. Then she did what she always did: she shrugged her shoulders and crossed her arms, using her palms to stroke and hug herself as if replacing her mother's embrace. Then she hopped and skipped along to join her friends, whistling a nursery rhyme.

'You silly, naughty girls—go away and don't come back. If you do I'll kill you!' Renee's mother Joy screamed, chasing the three girls out of her house. They giggled and ran out to the gravel road. Thick white moustaches of sugar grains extended round their pink mouths, ending like thin beards on their babyish chins.

It was mid-afternoon on a December day. The girls had been playing outside before the winter sunset, before the drop in temperature and darkness forced them indoors. The crisp fresh air and their vigorous games had whetted their appetites, so Renee had hatched the fine plan of inviting them to her house while her mother was out taking in the washing from the veranda. Renee had spotted her on the roof trying to tame the white sheets billowing in the wind.

She decided this was a perfect moment to treat her friends to their favourite snack. They crept into the kitchen and Renee cut thick rough chunks of fresh white bread. She sprinkled these with water from the tap and then dusted sugar generously on top. The girls grabbed these delicacies, crossed the corridor and tried to sneak out through the balcony door.

Suddenly they heard Joy behind them, screaming as she stood in the corridor holding her laundry basket. Sugar was crunching underneath her slippers as she moved in with her washing. When she realised what the three had done to her clean floor, she nearly dropped the basket.

'Renee, didn't I tell you that this is not the house for *marenda?*' she yelled. 'In this house, we eat only around the table, do you hear me? And we always use plates.'

But the girls had disappeared, laughing, leaving Joy in a rage.

Joy was the most house-proud lady in Portovecchio. She was so particular that life for her daughter and husband consisted of her constant nagging. She nagged even in anticipation of possible future mess or untidiness. Joy was tall, nearly five feet seven. She had a huge bosom and her undefined waistline was sited immediately below her breasts. There she rested her skirts and tied her belts or apron strings, as tightly as possible. Such fastening made her feel secure. She kept her floors well-polished, shiny. Her thick Anatolian carpets were shaken well every day, and washed with plenty of water and vinegar once a year. There was no hiding-place for mites; there was no room for even the tiniest speck of dust.

The sugar the girls dropped drove her insane. After resting the basket with the washing on her wonderful mock-Louis XV sofa, she got out a mop and started rubbing and wiping the floor. She hoped to absorb every last grain of sugar, restoring the floor to its pristine state.

'These girls are out of control. Can't they go and eat somewhere else?' she muttered. '*Marenda, marenda:* that's all they care about.'

Food was such a messy affair. As far as Joy was concerned, food and eating were in the same class as sex. To her, both activities were necessary, unavoidable—but messy. Everything always had to be cleared up afterwards. She had to do extra washing-up and rubbing. 'Childbirth is such a clumsy affair,' she always declared with great authority when an audience was at hand. Many in Portovecchio wondered how she had consented to produce a child.

For the girls, *marenda* was the best meal of the day. They didn't have to sit at the table and eat with any regard to either table manners or rules. It was a meal that they could munch on while playing, talking, reading or walking.

Marenda in Kerkyra is a snack-break *extraordinaire*. Everyone loves such snacks, which can in some ways be compared to English elevenses. People didn't eat sandwiches or breakfast in those days; they simply ate *marenda,* good, chunky, tasty, heavenly *marenda.* There were various types, all of them deeply embedded in the soul of all the people of Portovecchio.

The first *marenda* was the cheese-pie type. These pies were sold in the streets from a little portable metal box heated with hot ashes. They cost scarcely one drachma each. Cheese-pies are little triangular parcels wrapped in delicious crispy, greasy *filo* pastry filled with feta cheese. A good dose of semolina was often added in order to reduce the cost of production. They were sold by vendors who walked around the streets calling out: 'Cheese-pies, hot and fresh, one drachma each—come along, not many left.' They were sold in the mornings fresh from the ovens, and by lunchtime there *weren't* many left.

These cheese-pies were particularly popular with school-children, but office workers welcomed them too. After all, they had spent between six and twelve years in education eating them at eleven o'clock each morning, so how could they possibly give them up in adulthood? They were more or less addicted, and ate them until their dying day. Advice from doctors that cheese-pies should be avoided, especially by those suffering from high blood pressure, was ignored. As a result, it could be assumed that the high rate of strokes among people in Kerkyra in later life could have been prevented if everyone had reduced their cheese-pie intake.

The pies had to be fresh. If the vendor was unscrupulous and was selling the previous day's leftover pies re-warmed, those who ate them could be afflicted with a most unwelcome dose of the trots.

The second type of *marenda* was brown bread drenched with olive oil and covered with a thick layer of tomato paste. In Portovecchio there was a bakery run by a family of Armenian immigrants from Asia Minor, who produced heavenly bread. In Portovecchio's fragrances to be enjoyed, the aroma of the daily bread baking, blended with the smell of the salt sea, was at the top of the list.

Marenda which required bread always demanded the freshly-baked sort from the immigrant bakery. The two Armenian brothers, their youngest cousin and their mother, were the nicest people possible. In Portovecchio they were well-known and the locals looked up to them. They had seen the world, albeit in unfortunate circumstances, and were genteel and charming: 'refined'. These were the characteristics of most of the refugees who had arrived in such tragic circumstances from the depths of Anatolia, after the Asia Minor disaster. In contrast with the Portovecchians, they weren't garrulous. They were discreet, calm and silent. They had soft voices and the sad faces of persecution. What could they utter, after all, considering the horrors they had seen?

It was obvious that the family had been much better educated than the average Portovecchian, and they addressed everybody with respect, using a polite form. Their Greek vocabulary was not extensive and they spoke with a strong Armenian accent.

The Tzaroujian brothers ran the bakery efficiently and with great success. They didn't bake the bread themselves, but had men working the hot ovens. Rumour had it that in Anatolia the family had been rich and distinguished, but that they had lost everything, and the people here were the remaining members of an extended family. Only these few had survived the scimitar of the Turk.

Portovecchians often wondered how they had managed to bury their sorrows. They never mentioned them. The mother spent her free time doing exquisite embroidery, the young cousin was constantly flirting with the local girls, and the two brothers searched in vain for two good Armenian girls to marry. They all worked hard and were building their fortune again, slowly and steadily.

Apart from selling delicious bread, the Tzaroujians offered another invaluable service. They took in any dish that required baking and that people had prepared in the mornings for their lunch, and cooked it for them. Hardly any Portovecchians had the luxury of their own ovens at home. So each morning they entrusted their baking dishes, full of the day's meal, to the bakery, and the care of Mrs Tzaroujian. At lunchtime they picked it up, beautifully baked under her supervision, on the way home from work.

Each morning and lunchtime, the main road of Portovecchio witnessed an interesting procession of people carrying baking tins, going back and forth with roast chickens and roast potatoes; potatoes on their own in lemon and oregano, sprinkled with plenty of salt and pepper; stuffed tomatoes, aubergines and green peppers; pasta with lamb; roast lamb or pork with potatoes; summer vegetables in tomato sauce; *pastitso*; fish baked with tomatoes; fish baked with garlic and potatoes; *moussaka*–and many, many other delicious dishes.

I leave it to your imagination to savour the enticing and unforgettable smells of Portovecchio.

Two types of bread were available from the Tzaroujians', both delicious and in great demand for the *marenda*: white and brown. The brown was referred to as *black bread*. Both types came as round loaves, long loaves and rings, all at one drachma for two pounds, the same price as the daily newspaper, a little cheese-pie, and slightly more than a couple of pounds of fresh tomatoes or the bus ticket to town.

Another form of *marenda* was Blossom's favourite: a huge chunk of fresh bread accompanied with a sprinkle of olive oil. A large white raw onion was eaten with it. The town dwellers didn't eat this type of *marenda*. This was the favourite snack of 'uncouth peasants'. People like Tony directed their appetites away from the odour of garlic and onion as much as possible, regardless of how much they craved it. Only on 25 March, the holiday celebrating both Independence Day and the Assumption of the Virgin Mary, when custom dictated the consumption of the traditional garlic sauce with fried dried cod, did the people of the town force themselves to eat smelly garlic.

Blossom, as a born-and-bred peasant, adored her oniony *marenda*, insisting that it was the best possible snack at eleven o'clock every day. This drove Tony mad and Louisa even further away.

The smell of onion and garlic reminded Tony of his daily trip to the hospital, so many years before. The smell used to suffocate him then and it was destroying him now. Blossom appalled him, and he never went near her. Sex was never an issue between Tony and his new wife, so neither of them tried at any time to attract the other. Good smells and bad smells were really equally unimportant, since sex was non-existent in their shared lives. When both of them lay in bed at night, the space between them was more divisive than the Iron Curtain.

The Portovecchians' favourite *marendas* were made with fresh bread and tomato paste. From time to time people liked a chunk of fresh black bread accompanied with either creamy feta or *lefkaditiko* salami. They ate and ate and ate.

The children's favourites were the cheese-pies and bread with sugar. The first kept their stomachs full during school hours, while the second gave their mouths the opportunity of the sweet interplay between tongue, palate and taste-buds. Louisa, Maria and Renee loved aggravating the adults by spreading sugar grains on the floor, so much so that when they grew a bit older and went to high school, they would sometimes sprinkle sugar on the classroom floors. It was such fun! Madame who taught them French used to sway in for their French lessons wearing her outmoded high Parisian heels. She was myopic and could never understand why her feet went *crunch-crunch* every time she entered that particular classroom.

Out in the chill of that winter afternoon of 10 December, after Joy had chased them away, the girls were joined by Mamee the cat. She emerged through the gate of Louisa's house with her usual slow, arrogant and confident walk, her little bell tinkling as it dangled from her neck. She had put on a lot of weight since her owners had deserted her. Most of the neighbours were over-generous in feeding her, in an effort to keep her away from their kitchens.

Louisa went down on her knees and begged her to approach. Since the summer the cat had got used to her and, knowing that Louisa was a good source of food, accepted her cuddles and affection without fuss. The cat walked up slowly and rubbed herself against Louisa's thin legs. The girl tried to give her some bread and sugar, but the cat refused it. Louisa then picked her up and kissed her. The three girls, ignoring the chill of the late afternoon, sat on the curb pretending the cat was their baby. She looked as if she loved this human touch and purred and purred.

Cats' thoughts are as unknown to humans as certainty or knowledge of what follows after death. The Portovecchians kept feeding the cat, summoning her or kicking her. Nobody could know what she was thinking. Was she missing her owners? Was she glad that they had gone and that she was free to roam around? Could she discriminate between generosity and meanness? Had she absorbed the significance of Theodora's rape up in the cemetery or Zoë's pain in the heart? Did she know that Louisa was the loneliest girl in Portovecchio? Who knows? The only thing we know for certain is that in spite of their frequent feelings of irritation many people loved the cat and found comfort in stroking her, in running their fingers through her silky thick black-and-white coat, in talking to her in solitude and kissing her. She was also useful for getting rid of the occasional rat.

As the girls were playing mother with Mamee, Theodora emerged from Maria's house. She had finished her day's work and was leaving for home. She was dressed all in black, and had recently—just like the cat—put on a lot of weight.

She greeted the girls sadly. Their presence reminded her of little Alice's absence. It was almost six weeks since the funeral and over three months since Father Anthony had assaulted her in the cemetery. Theodora knew that she was with child. Luckily she was not feeling nauseous any more—but how long could she keep her secret? She could see Father Anthony's house across the road next to the church. The two buildings, close to each other and linked by an average-sized garden full of fruit trees, were shrouded in a thick veil of Christianity. As far as buildings go they were without doubt the biggest in the neighbourhood: churches almost universally seem to be substantial land-owners and money-grabbers. What does God have to say when his palaces of indulgence stand so superior, full of candles and comfort, among the shanty-towns of the world? Pity the people who depend on churches and believe in their holiness.

Warm light poured from the kitchen window of Father Anthony's house, framed with little lace curtains. Outside on the street it was getting dark and really chilly. 'They're all there, children, wife and all,' Theodora thought, and tears rose to her eyes. She was older than Maria, Renee and Louisa, but still technically a child–yet she had never played as they did. From the age of ten she'd had to work. It seemed as if she had been born a grown-up woman.

'Hey, Theodora–you're just the person I want,' came a voice from the balcony of Renee's house. Joy stood there, tall and erect as an ancient column. On her head she had a velour leopard-skin turban, and round her shoulders she had placed a big purple cashmere shawl to protect her from the December cold.

'Hello–what do you want me for?' Theodora responded abruptly.

'It's about tomorrow. I need you to come and help me. I must clean the house, and I have to cook *pastitsada*. Have you forgotten? The day after tomorrow it's Saint Spiridion's day, my Spiros' name day.'

Spiros was Joy's husband, Renee's father and Zoë's brother. 'I'll speak to Emilia, and ask her to give you the day off,' Joy said loudly and with authority from the balcony.

'As you like,' Theodora responded indifferently and, greeting the girls coolly, she started walking down the hill towards her house.

'Maria, go and call your Gran to come out. I want to talk to her,' Joy said, with authority. Emilia and Joy had been friends for years, so they had an agreement between them to share Theodora as the need arose. Her wishes barely came into it.

'I can't go now—I'm busy,' Maria said, preoccupied with the cat.

'I asked you to go, but you're so rude and impertinent. Don't bother yourself. Renee, can you go then, please? I must speak to Emilia.'

Renee was also indifferent. 'Go yourself, Mother,' she said.

'I'll go.' Louisa jumped up, dropping the cat from her lap to the ground. She ran to summon Emilia.

'There she goes,' the other two girls murmured under their breaths. 'Always the goody-goody.' But they didn't really care.

Emilia came out of her house, followed by Louisa.

'So you need Theodora tomorrow? You can have her, but I'd better warn you that there's something wrong with the girl. We don't know what to make of it. Do talk to her and see if you can find out.'

'It's because of Alice's death,' said Joy. 'It's upset them all. But they knew she was dying, after all. They had ten years to get used to it. I can't see why it's taken them so much by surprise. I must get up early tomorrow; I have so much to do. I must finish the ironing, clean the windows, change the beds, shake the carpets, and then cook *pastitsada*.'

Darkness was falling fast and the chill in the air made staying out of doors unpleasant. In December the days in Portovecchio are short and the nights very long. Emilia went back indoors, ordering Maria to follow her. Joy told Renee to stop wasting time and come indoors too. Louisa, gently picking up Mamee, made for her own house.

Joy left her balcony like an empress in retreat, a ruler fully aware of her power and strength. She shut the windows and entered her neat and spotless kingdom.

Every year she was in two minds about December. She loved the cold weather that gave her the excuse to light her precious cast-iron stove, which crackled with burning wood. She loved the many saints' days that gave her the excuse to clean and clean and clean. But she hated the fact that people visited each other during these holy days, spreading such dirt and untidiness. Sticky glasses had to be washed; mud had be cleaned from the floor; ashtrays full of foul cigarette ash had to be emptied and soaked; windows had to be opened in order to get rid of all the human smells. But the day after, Joy always had a grand excuse to start cleaning again, something that gave her a real thrill. She loved nothing better than to see her house clean, tidy and shining. When everything was done she would take a bath and sit on her mock-Louis XV sofa, turban and all, and listen to her radio. If only everyone living in this house would disappear, leaving her to indulge in the order she pursued and adored!

Louisa arrived home lovingly cradling the cat.

'Where have you been?' her father asked.

'Out with my friends.'

'Your mouth is smeared with sugar. Haven't I told you time and time again that sugar is bad for you? Blossom, take her and wash her face. And that cat, get her out of my house. She attacked the sardines only half an hour ago. Get her out!' Tony yelled in a loud and frightening voice.

Louisa let the cat go. Mamee ran like lightning out of the house. She had been kicked out of there only a short while ago. In this house she wasn't loved. To Tony and Blossom, she was a thief. They always kicked her out. The only place she could find refuge was with Louisa in her den. There she was fed with milk and biscuits and other little catty goodies.

Blossom stood up from her chair. She took Louisa gently by the hand, to wash her. Louisa abruptly pulled her hand away. 'I can do it myself.'

The atmosphere in the house was as heavy as the darkness outside. The long winter evenings were the worst time in their new home in Portovecchio. Tony and Blossom had nothing to say to each other, or rather *he* had a lot to say: orders and orders and more orders, never-ending. Blossom in return did everything without complaining. As long as she had good food to eat, was away from her sister-in-law, and was left alone to spin her wool, she was content.

That day there had been an outburst from Tony, caused by the cat's stealing. You couldn't say that the couple argued, because in order to have an argument two people have to interact. The shouting was always a monologue from Tony followed by silence from Blossom. His loud anger was a release of his frustration. He was full of remorse for his mistakes. He recognised that his life had been ruined again. The first time it had been destroyed by a death, the second time by a marriage.

Louisa, having half-cleaned the sugar off her face, pulled her favourite chair away from the dining table and placed it next to their radio, a pre-War German model. Every night at six o'clock she loved listening to the first-ever soap. Called *The Concierge,* it explored the daily lives of the residents of a modern block of flats in booming Athens. Louisa imagined that she also lived there, just as she had in her Aunt Camilla's beautiful apartment.

The cat steals, eats and sleeps well, while Joy cooks…

When Maria and Renee went home, they felt they were entering warm, welcoming shelters. These were clean and ordered houses, and nothing in them had changed since the day they were born. The people around them were part of each other, one flesh and one blood. Louisa would have loved to be part of something similar. She constantly tried to please her new neighbours, and impress them so they would start liking her enough to include her in their family life. She longed to be invited into their homes. There she could share the warmth of their families, the tranquillity. She knew too little to suspect that pain also existed under their roofs, pain caused by John's political ideas and Joy's yearning for her husband Spiro, who had been absent for a long time, working as a captain on one of the boats of the Hellenic Merchant Navy.

Joy's pride in her home pleased Louisa. She felt the reproduction furniture imported by Spiro from abroad was much better than either Blossom's or her father's possessions. Louisa was too young to realise that her feelings towards the interior decoration of her house had more to do with her mother's everlasting absence than with Blossom's ideas about home-making.

After taking many orders from Joy, Theodora returned to her family and went straight to bed. She felt worn out by hard work. Peter, George and Adelaide were busy repairing the fishing nets and hardly noticed her.

The next day was the eve of Saint Spiridion's day. On every street corner of the Old Town of Kerkyra a male cook in white overalls and a tall white hat stood serving *loukoumades*, traditional little doughnuts. In front of each cook a stove had been placed, with a huge cauldron on top, full of simmering olive oil. On a table at the side was a big clay basin where the *loukoumades* batter had been mixed. Holding huge ladles, the cooks spooned the thick batter out of the clay basin a spoonful at a time and dropped it into the hot oil, carefully and expertly. When the *loukoumades* had turned crisp and golden, and while the customers waited patiently, the cooks collected their payment of a few drachmas. The piping-hot *loukoumades* were sprinkled with sugar and cinnamon and served in a brown bag.

They were among the many joys that Saint Spiridion's name day brought to everyone on the island. The church dedicated to him, housing his serene corpse, was located in the heart of the Old Town. On 11 December every year it was decorated with flowers and laurels and beautifully lit. Everyone was welcome to come in. People visited the church in droves, as they found it difficult to come to terms with the injustices of God. They were convinced that Saint Spiridion represented their best hope by far. They always prayed to him and asked him to put right God's injustices. By executing many miracles through the years, Saint Spiridion had become the Patron Saint of Kerkyra. Whether people were atheists or believers, everybody believed without hesitation in the holiness of the saint. The miracles were solid proof of that power. Sicknesses and deformities that God had bestowed, Saint Spiridion often cured or put right.

No child went to take exams without first kissing the saint's feet, as he lay calmly in his open casket. Most of Kerkyra's children did well at school. Was this because of these visits, or mere coincidence? Saint Spiridion's celebrations lasted two whole days. There was no school during this time.

The housewives prepared themselves in the manner they knew best: they cleaned and washed with enormous enthusiasm, competing among themselves to be the one with the best house. Their ambition was that the day would dawn full of cleanliness, whitewash and good food. Saint Spiridion's day was a joyous one.

Not everyone looked forward to it, however. Theodora had to face a day of hard work for Joy. Theodora had lost faith in Saint Spiridion soon after Alice was born. He had done nothing for her poor sister, whose stomach had just become more and more bloated. And as for the present, Saint Spiridion had completely failed to strike Father Anthony dead.

Theodora arrived at Joy's house almost half an hour before she was due. The knowledge that she had a child inside her was keeping her awake at night. She left her home without even a cup of coffee, in order to avoid having to talk with her family. Facing them every day was becoming unbearable.

She found Joy already up and about, but still in her dressing gown, worn on top of her pink-and-white nightdress. Joy always did her housework dressed like that. Washing herself, dressing up, combing her hair with great care and applying her thick, bright make-up took place only after all the chores had been done. Then she would be perfect for the rest of the day.

She opened the door for Theodora and ordered her to wash her hands and put on an enormous plastic apron. 'Come on, you. We have to cook the *pastitsada* first,' she said in her strong, authoritarian, but still affectionate voice.

They entered the kitchen together. The aluminium saucepans had been polished so meticulously that they appeared like endless mirrors, reflecting all the objects round the room.

Every shelf had been lined with a well-pressed sheet of newspaper, so that when the shelves were cleaned, only the newspapers had to be changed. Four pounds of beef, in one piece, were resting on a big platter.

'I'll tell you what to do, and you listen and cook,' Joy told Theodora. Joy hated cooking. She would rather polish all her copper, brass and silver.

In her seventeen years of life, Theodora had cooked *pastitsada* hundreds of times, either for her family or for Emilia. She loved eating it, too–but not today. Her stomach felt as if she were floating out on rough seas. She washed her hands carefully and dried them on the crisp, white towel hanging from a hook next to the kitchen sink.

Theodora liked Joy enormously, in spite of her manic attitude to housework. Joy regularly helped her family, either by buying George's freshly-caught fish, or by passing on clothes for Alice, Adelaide and Theodora. In her free time Theodora liked to visit Joy and sit next to her on the ornate sofa, where she would be doing her nails. She would offer Theodora advice on taking care of hers. In spite of her youth, Theodora's nails were fragile and rough. Housework never gave them a chance to grow and look elegant.

Joy would give her nail polish and every so often the end of a lipstick. Spiro was a great supplier of bottles of perfume and other exotic cosmetics. Joy knew how much poor Theodora liked all these luxuries, so she passed them on to cheer her up.

'My God,' Joy thought to herself, 'today she looks particularly miserable.' Aloud she said: 'Theodora, listen. Take the meat, wash it and cut it into portions.' Theodora did as she was told.

Joy forged on. 'There are the pounds of meat, so you must use six big white onions. They're in the basket above the fridge: help yourself. The grater is in the first drawer to the left of the sink. Garlic—you need four cloves—is in that little dish next to the onions. Use the mortar and pestle to crush the garlic. You have to bring them in from the yard. Careful you don't drop the mortar; it's old and precious.'

Joy said all this in a slow, calm voice as she sat on a chair by the kitchen table, vigorously polishing her silver and brass. Theodora knew all this information by heart. What did Signora Joy think: that she was stupid?

She obediently cut the meat, peeled the onions and garlic and then went out to bring in the mortar and pestle. The cold air penetrated her thin clothing. She spotted them next to a big pot of dead hydrangeas. She picked them up, hoping that the weight might force the child out of her stomach—but no such luck. Instead, what with the smell of the onions and garlic, the cold air and her early rising, she felt nauseous. She put the mortar down again and sat on the kerb by the little green gate that led to the path to the church and the cemetery.

Dark thoughts overwhelmed her. The inside of her stomach felt as if it were packed with ice. She had to vomit—but where? She got up, opened the gate and ran out up the little hill behind the church. The cemetery was completely empty at this time of the day. Some graves had dead flowers on them, and others extinguished candles.

Theodora couldn't hold back any longer. She retched and threw up right into a freshly-dug open hole.

'That's something—at least, I didn't soil Signora Joy's garden,' she thought, and wiped her mouth with the corner of her skirt, underneath the stiff, cold plastic apron. Then slowly she plucked up courage and walked the short distance back to Joy's garden. She heard her strong voice calling: 'Theodora, where are you? Come on, girl, we have so much to do.'

Theodora picked up the mortar and pestle and went into the kitchen. She felt completely unable to carry on cooking.

'Please, Signora Joy, I can't do it,' she begged. 'My stomach is funny today. Please let me polish the brass and silver instead. I'm really good at that,' she pleaded.

Joy stared hard at her. 'You're pregnant.' She said it without thinking, then was shocked by her own words. What had made her say that? She knew nothing about the girl's relationship with her sailor.

'Are you?' she enquired more gently, expecting Theodora to deny the accusation.

'Yes, I am,' the girl replied, looking straight into her eyes.

'But we all thought your bad temper was due to Alice's death. What have you done, you silly, stupid girl? Have you no self-control?'

Theodora wasn't listening. She placed the mortar and pestle next to the raw, red, juicy pieces of beef and the tear-inducing onions. Then she pulled a little stool from underneath the table and sat down.

'It was Father Anthony,' she said simply.

'What! Are you in your right mind?' Joy was shocked, but not particularly surprised. She had known since they were young that Anthony was a lecher and a brute. He had *how many* children? She couldn't think—a lot, anyway. He had fancied Zoë for years, and wasn't he sleeping with Fat Foni?

'My God, how did it happen?'

'Nothing to do with me,' Theodora pleaded. She started crying. 'It was up there in the cemetery after the fiesta.'

Her crying intensified. Joy got up and, with her hands still covered in Brasso, embraced the girl tenderly. With affection she kissed her on the top of her head. One didn't need a doctorate in forensics to understand what must have happened.

'The bastard!' Joy said in a flat voice. 'Don't worry about the cooking, I'll do that. Just wipe your tears before others see you. Then take my chair and do the polishing. I'll cook today.'

Theodora did what she was told.

'What are you going to do about the baby?'

'I don't know–I'm lost,' she said, in a whisper.

'Have you told the monster yet?'

'No, I can't. He said that if I spoke to anybody, he would excommunicate me, curse me, even kill me. Please don't say I told you.'

Joy turned back to the sink and bent her head. 'I'll cook the *pastitsada*. What do we need next? Just keep quiet and I'll think of something. Don't worry, please–just calm down. I'll take care of it.'

What made Theodora confide in Joy? She had no idea. She had to tell somebody in that particular moment of desperation. She was only seventeen, after all. Joy wasn't family and her relative wealth separated her from the rest of Portovecchio. Her authoritative loud voice made people respect her. At that moment, Theodora had felt it was the only thing she could do. She trusted Joy out of instinct and necessity. She felt that by talking to this powerful woman, she might gain help. Joy might be able to assist her in a way that nobody else could.

Silence fell in the kitchen. The silver, copper and brass polishing went on noiselessly. Joy pretended she was cooking but she was actually doing nothing. She needed a few minutes to catch her breath. Then she brought a big heavy flat-bottomed saucepan out of the cupboard and started heating it, in deadly silence.

Theodora went on quietly cleaning the brass.

'I must concentrate hard. I can't remember the ingredients. Where is the cookery book, my old standby?' Then she did what no honourable home cook would ever do. She started following the recipe from this book. Today she just couldn't think at all coherently.

She followed the recipe step by step, very clearly repeating the instructions to herself out loud, as if she were a teacher giving dictation to a child.

'Grate the onion to a pulp.' She did that to the point where she nearly grated her own fingers. 'Put two spoonfuls of olive oil in the pan.' She spilt the oil and managed to put too much olive oil in the heavy-bottomed saucepan. 'Add the meat.' She added the meat, and fried it through quickly. 'Add the onions.' She added the onions and the mashed-up garlic which she'd pounded viciously in the mortar with the pestle. Once these three ingredients had been fried and browned well she turned away from the cookery book which had received many splashes of hot olive oil. How can one read and cook at the same time? She added lots of peeled tomatoes, two tablespoons of tomato paste, two cups of red wine, two teaspoons of sugar, three cinnamon sticks, ten cloves, almost a handful of nutmeg and another of caraway seeds. These gave it her own extra touch. Then she sprinkled on salt and pepper.

Unfortunately, without realising it, so preoccupied was she with Theodora's predicament, that she added far too much salt. Nobody was going to enjoy this *pastitsada* at the celebratory lunch the next day. In the history of Kerkyra, nobody had ever thought of *pastitsada* as a dish that could be ruined. But it was. It was Joy's first inedible *pastitsada*.

She pulled a clean handkerchief out of her apron pocket, since her eyes were filling with tears. But it wasn't just the onions. Anthony's wickedness interfered with her cooking to such an extent that she completely forgot to peel the onions under a running tap. Before she put the lid on the heavy-bottomed saucepan, she added a little water. She covered it and then made a mental note that she'd have to let the meat cook for quite a while, every so often remembering to check the liquid and adding water as necessary. The sauce had to be thick, red and tasty, whatever happened. It had to be sufficient to coat the spaghetti she would serve everybody the next day.

The trick with *pastitsada* is always to cook it, ever so slowly, the day before it is eaten. It tastes delicious the day after it is cooked. On the following day, just before lunch, Joy would boil a packet of macaroni Misko *al dente* and stir the sauce over it. Then she would serve it with plenty of grated parmesan.

Louisa's bedroom faced the uphill gravel road, and opposite she could see Renee's house. The priest's house and her friend's home were next to each other, separated by an alley. Renee's house was the taller of the two. It was a two-storey residence, something unusual among the humble cottages of Portovecchio. Its main entrance door, painted green and white, was at the front of the house, a few steps up from the gravel road. To its side, and halfway up the alley were a few steps leading to a second door, another entrance. Entering through this door meant going through Renee's bedroom.

It was in this alley and on those steps that Louisa saw Theodora lying, as if asleep. It was the night of 11 December, after all the housework had been done, and the *pastitsades* had been placed in the larder to mature. A nightmare had awoken Louisa, the same one that had awoken her repeatedly since her mother's death. She would dream that she was outdoors, in the dark, looking up at a starry sky. Then suddenly and with the speed of lightning the stars and the moon would collide. The force of this collision would bring about the most horrendous explosion. The sky would be lit up as if full of fireworks, and the stars and the moon would turn into fiery splinters. Louisa would be rained upon by millions of fiery sparks that wouldn't burn her but make her freeze. The Universe would become full of the freezing rain of fire splinters falling with great speed from the black sky to the dark earth. An enormous rough hole would be formed in the sky, an entrance to the far-and-beyond. The cold rain of fire would be transformed on earth into black-robed monks walking silently in an open space, carrying tall white candles. They would move slowly away from Louisa, leaving her alone. They would proceed as in a parade up a long, dark road. Slowly they would be transformed again, this time into dark shadows, black silhouettes on the wall next to Louisa's bed.

She would wake soaked in sweat, and would run to her bedroom window. Blossom had told her that when she woke from such nightmares the best thing she could do was go to the window and open the shutters to look at the moon. This would reassure her that there were no black holes in the sky, and that everything was normal. The fresh air would make her forget the nightmare.

Blossom was right. This advice actually worked, in spite of the fact that Louisa would have preferred to run into her parents' bedroom and cuddle up in her mother's arms.

On this night of 11 December, she opened the shutters wide. The cold of the night penetrated the room. Louisa took a deep breath and lifted her head to look at the sky. It was full of stars. There was Venus, and there was Hermes. It was so bitterly cold that now the nightmare had gone, she was ready to retreat back to the warmth of her bed.

Then she caught sight of what looked like a heap of old rugs lying in the alley, on the steps leading to Renee's house. The moonlight was falling gently on to them. Looking more closely, Louisa saw that they were shaped as if a human body was entangled in them. Who could it be? she puzzled. She continued staring out the wide-open window.

Suddenly Mamee the cat jumped from within the front garden bushes on to her window sill. She sat there, looking lazily at Louisa. The cat's eyes sparkled in the dark. Louisa started stroking her, and the cat purred.

Louisa had an idea. She left the cat on the window sill and turned back to her bedroom. She found her little stool, which she put against the wall. Then she climbed up to the window sill and by going leg-first over the parapet, she jumped outside. Her bare feet felt the cold cement of the front yard.

Mamee followed her. Although she was only in her flannel nightdress, Louisa felt no cold at all. Her curiosity was guiding her. She crossed the gravel road and with bravery well beyond her ten years, went to investigate who the figure in the rugs could be. Louisa's courage was based on her deeply-held assumption that there was no evil in Kerkyra. In those days, no homeless people used the street as their beds. She thought that it must be Renee, whom her cruel mother had kicked out of her bedroom because of the incident with the sugar.

She approached the heap slowly. As she came closer she suddenly recognised Theodora's shape, and then her head, which was protruding from the rugs. She was lying there in a heap, asleep in the middle of the night, in the moonlight. Why on earth was she sleeping there? Her home was only a little further down the road.

'Theodora! Theodora—it's me, Louisa. Why are you here? Why aren't you sleeping in your own bed?' Louisa stood there, the cat next to her, both of them waiting for an answer.

Theodora stirred and then, opening her eyes, she pulled her ragged white blanket away from her head and looked up at Louisa, surprised.

'What are you doing here? Go back—let me sleep.'

'Are you mad? This isn't a bed. It's freezing. Go home.'

'No, I can't. I'm in trouble. I don't want to see them any more. I'm pregnant. I have a baby in my stomach. Now you know—but do you understand what this means? Everybody will know soon, including my parents. It wasn't so bad before, when it didn't show. But now I can't sleep in my house or go near the place. I must die here.'

Tears were rolling down Theodora's face, and Louisa could see her tummy was certainly sticking out more than usual, since she was lying down. Louisa thought of Alice and her distinctive stomach. The idea of pregnancy didn't frighten her. Why should it? Both Louisa and Theodora were too young to absorb the implications rationally, too young to solve this universal problem.

'A baby, a baby,' she thought. 'But where is its father?' This was the first thing Louisa thought to ask.

'Oh, come and sit down, both of you,' Theodora begged Louisa and the cat. First Louisa sat next to her and then the cat jumped and sat on her lap.

'This is where I'm going to sleep until I die. Then everything will be all right,' said Theodora. 'My family won't want me in the house. They'll say that I'm a whore. Do you know what a whore is? I'm a whore. My boyfriend was a sailor doing his military service–but he's gone now.' She spoke as if she were reciting a poem. The tears had stopped and now she sounded drained of emotion.

'I'm so hungry; I had nothing to eat for supper. Go on, Louisa–go to your kitchen and get me something to eat. Please.'

The cat jumped from Louisa's lap onto Theodora's. She curled up there among the old rugs. Louisa got up and ran towards her house. She climbed in at the window again, ran through her bedroom, the hall and the dining room, and entered the kitchen. She opened the bread bin and got out half a loaf of black bread. Then she opened the larder, where she found a little dish with anchovies swimming in olive oil and vinegar. She emptied them into a small plastic box and carried them out to Theodora.

The three of them starting eating as if at a midnight feast.

While all this was going on, Renee, whose bed was just on the other side of the door, woke up. What were those strange noises and cat's meowing? She got out of bed and half-opened her door. Outside she saw Theodora, Louisa and Mamee eating away in the freezing night.

'A feast?' She opened the door wide. 'I want some too—but first come in, come in. Come and sit on my floor. It's warmer in here.'

Excited with the naughtiness and novelty of a midnight feast, Renee never thought to ask what was going on. The only thing she wanted was to have them all in her bedroom, to dip the bread in the oil and vinegar and eat the anchovies.

They all trooped in. Mamee placed herself comfortably on Renee's bed, while the other three sat cross-legged on the carpet. They ate, had a good laugh, and stroked the cat so much that she got fed up and left the room. Then the three of them fell soundly asleep on the floor.

The next morning the cheerful ringing of the bells from all the churches on the island woke the world to a joyful mood in spite of the bad weather. Everything had been prepared the day before. Clothes had been washed and pressed. Houses had been cleaned, cakes had been baked and holiday lunches had either been cooked in advance or were having the last touches put to them. The shops were closed. The workers, offered this little holiday in the middle of winter, were intending to sleep in to rest their exhausted bones.

Joy got up, and since it was such a holy day, and the name day of her seafaring husband, she didn't intend to indulge in her usual sweeping, dusting and mopping. Theodora's confession the previous day had also deprived her of a restful night's sleep. She yelled at Renee to get up, get dressed, and get ready for church. She had decided that they weren't going to go to

Saint Spiridion's church this morning, as she and Renee had done all the years her husband Spiro had been at sea with the ships. This year they would go to their local church. Saint Spiridion would understand and perhaps would give her a helping hand to solve Theodora's problem.

Joy had decided to go to Father Anthony's church and stare at him with piercing eyes while he was conducting the service. She would concentrate and pray hard at the same time, hoping that her meaningful gaze would kill him on the spot.

This wouldn't, of course, solve Theodora's problem. She wanted Saint Spiridion to help her find another solution entirely. She had been thinking about it all night and had formed a plan, although it was still very vague. She would go to the church in Portovecchio and then, when the service was over, she would send Renee to Zoë's to play with Maria and would get hold of that dreadful beast of a priest. She knew it was his custom to visit Fat Foni at the end of each service, before he went home to his ignorant, pathetic wife and his umpteen children. She would storm into Fat Foni's house and reveal the simpleton's deeds in front of her.

Joy started getting ready. She put on her bright red lipstick. She drew long, curvy lines above her dark brown eyes where her eyebrows had been before she had plucked them out. She puffed up her hair and showered it with hairspray that covered her entire head like a hard invisible helmet. Out of the wardrobe she got her new silk dress and cardigan and the most beautiful fur coat that Spiro had brought her from Vladivostock after one of his trips.

She put on the silk dress, taking care that her helmet of hair didn't get spoiled. She put on her cardigan carefully so that it wouldn't stretch and then she climbed on a chair and brought down from the top of her wardrobe a shoebox that contained the most beautiful stiletto shoes that money could buy.

Joy so loved to be the best-dressed woman in Portovecchio. She was full of pride that she was one of the few without a *morozo* to worry about. She didn't depend on giving her body to some other woman's husband in order to afford the nice things in life. She was proud of the fact that the honest money of her seafaring husband provided everything she needed.

She was searching for her handbag when she noticed that Renee hadn't yet emerged from her own bedroom. Balancing on her high stilettos she went to enter Renee's room. In the corridor in front of the half-opened door, Mamee was asleep on a little mat.

'How did you get in?' she said to the cat in a gentle voice. Then she opened the door wide, and with determination she entered her daughter's bedroom, which still had its shutters closed and was dark.

'Renee, get up! It's late!' she called, and feeling her way carefully, she walked to the window and opened the shutters wide. She was taken aback when, by daylight, she saw the three girls asleep on the carpet, surrounded by crumbs, leftover anchovies and oil and vinegar stains.

Her amazement was stronger than her reaction to the mess. She didn't get angry, as she would have in other circumstances. She looked at the three girls, who had only just stirred in their deep sleep at the noise and commotion she had caused. Theodora seemed not much older than the other two. Louisa, the little orphan newcomer, still had her eyes closed and was resting her head on Theodora's stomach. Renee slept as she always did, with her face squashed against the floor and her bottom sticking up in the air.

'Girls, girls– wake up! What's going on?' called Joy. The three of them jumped up with a shock and immediately realised that they were in for trouble. In their half-asleep state they were frightened. They didn't know what to expect. But Joy's voice sounded calm and kind, not angry, not nagging. They relaxed a little.

Joy proceeded to pick up the mess from the floor. She asked questions as if she wasn't bothered about what had happened during the night. Theodora lifted her heavy body from the floor, and with her head lowered and her glance directed beyond the window, said to Joy: 'Please don't make me go home or send me to Emilia's to work. Please keep me here.'

'You didn't go home last night, did you?' Joy stated, rather than asked.

Theodora ignored the question and sat back on the floor. The cat left the mat outside the room, walked confidently in, and settled on Theodora's old rug. Joy felt somewhat at a loss.

'Louisa, you go home before you're missed. You, Renee, get ready for church…' Then, on second thoughts, she added: 'No, don't come to church today. Since Theodora's here, you two stay and play. Eat and do whatever you like. I'll go to church on my own. We'll tell George and Adelaide that I invited you to sleep here, with Renee.'

Louisa left them without a word. She jumped and sang her usual tune all the way to her house. It was wet and cold outside. She put her arms around herself as always, hugging them the way she did when hard thinking was required.

The other two were delighted to be left behind in Mamee's company rather than being forced to go to church or outside into the cold. Mamee thought otherwise. She got up and followed Louisa, her source of milk and biscuits. Everyone else fed her with fish and more fish.

Chapter 8

Joy comes to the rescue, and trees are uprooted

*Her only dowry was the sea,
The best a man could have.
An empty chest. Her only dowry
The sea, the unspoilt sea!*

December 1956

Louisa found her window open, just as she had left it. She climbed over the sill and entered the warmth of her room. The cat jumped after her.

Slowly and timidly daylight was spreading over the island. Louisa clumsily closed the window behind her. She put back under her bed the little stool she had used to escape. Since it was raining outside, her nightclothes were damp. She had to find something dry. The day before, she had seen a pile of freshly washed and ironed clothes on a chair in the dining room. Hoping they would still be there, she quietly opened her bedroom door and tiptoed across the hall. She entered the room as quietly as the cat beside her.

The door leading to Tony and Blossom's bedroom was half-open. She could hear both of them snoring. She was relieved that they were still asleep, and that her adventure had gone unnoticed. They were lying with their backs turned to one another. Blossom's curly hair was sticking up in an unruly way and surrounded her large head on the pillow. On Tony's bedside table, a clock was ticking away the seconds. A pile of books lay on the floor. He would read at all hours of the day and night. Reading had become for him the best means of avoiding even the smallest communication with Blossom. A sour smell of tobacco hung over the room from an ashtray full of cigarette butts. There was also an empty glass still smelling of ouzo.

Tony's bedside light had been left on. Every night sleep caught him unawares as he read and smoked. Blossom, following him to bed, would extinguish his glowing cigarette with no sign of annoyance or impatience. She accepted all marital hardships with stoicism and the heroic expectation that nothing better was possible.

Even little Louisa recognised that sooner or later her father was bound to burn the house down. She sometimes hoped that he would, and that one day they would all vanish, that her nightmares would become reality, that lightning would strike and fire would engulf them all.

Suddenly she felt nausea overcome her. She had to throw up. She ran to the lavatory, knelt in front of the toilet bowl, and vomited. It must have been those midnight anchovies–or maybe it was Blossom and Tony in bed together that had turned her stomach upside down.

Mamee had followed her and stood next to her, staring with her big blue eyes, now and then giving a tiny cry. Eventually Louisa got up from the cold floor, and wiped her mouth with some paper she pulled from the holder. Feeling a bit wobbly, she returned to the dining room.

She grabbed some dry clothes from the chair and retreated towards her bedroom. She did not realise that the cat had stopped following her. Mamee had run back into Tony and Blossom's bedroom and jumped, uninvited, on to their bed. She settled down between them.

Blossom screamed and Tony cursed. Louisa quickly ran into her bedroom, pulling the door shut behind her.

Saint Spiridion's day began with thin rain. As it progressed the rain became heavier and the wind blew with all its might. The temperature fell to eight degrees.

Joy found it difficult to keep her umbrella open on her short walk to the church. Since she was wearing her very expensive stilettos, she tried hard to avoid the puddles. This was almost impossible. Stilettos were not made for the gravel roads of Portovecchio. By the time she got to the church, in spite of the fact that it was almost next door, her beautiful fur coat from Vladivostock was soaking wet from the rain. Her helmet of hair had collapsed slightly. Perspiration mixed with rain dripped down her forehead. When the Soviet furriers produced their coats they hardly had a Mediterranean climate in mind.

When Joy paid her visits to church—not very often—she made sure she arrived towards the end of the service. She found churches depressing, macabre. She couldn't stand or comprehend the long-winded mumbo-jumbo of the old ecclesiastical Hellenic language. As soon as she entered a church, particularly this one, her own parish church, she thought of funerals. This was the church of her parents' funerals. For weddings and christenings most Portovecchians favoured the cathedral in the town. It was bigger, lighter and friendlier.

Joy remembered that the last time she had come to this church had been for little Alice's funeral. How sad it had all been! Joy mostly used churches when she was desperate about some issue in her life, when she had to pray and ask God for a favour. If humans were really happy, without a care in the world, would they go to church? she often wondered. She didn't really want to be here. If she had a choice she would be somewhere else.

The rain which had started about six o'clock that morning showed no signs of ceasing. In the summer, when she could, Joy would always be outdoors. Living by the sea was like being part of a big wholesome funfair. There was always something to do: swimming, fishing, boating, enjoying the landscape, breathing in the salt and the spray, bargaining with the fishermen over the price of their catch. Even when the sea was rough the view was good. It was amazing how the immense blue canvas could catch your eye at any time, Joy thought. Just admiring its constant changes was an antidote to misery. It revitalised her spirit.

Of course, when the sea became furious the women would be down on their knees praying tearfully for the safe return of their men. Still, most of the time the constant movement of the waters of the Ionian Archipelago worked for the Portovecchians like the best anti-depressant in the world.

Joy comes to the rescue, and trees are uprooted

On that 12 December, Joy was sure that the only place she would find Anthony was at the church. She had been amazed by Theodora's revelation of the previous day. Poor girl! Joy's anger at the priest was spurring her on. If it weren't for the fact that she had to talk to this satyr posing as a Christian, she might not have emerged from her house at all. Perhaps she would have gone instead to the church of Saint Spiridion in the Old Town.

When she was at any church, Joy never used a pew. She was in the habit of standing erect between the candle stand and the door, the best place to be to get out first at the end of the service. On this day she ventured a bit further inside since the cold was bothering her. Wet from the rain and perspiration caused by her coat, she thought she might catch pneumonia.

As she entered, Father Anthony was coming towards the end of the Gospel reading. Joy tried to listen but it didn't really interest her. When he finished, he went up to the pulpit and started his sermon. It was full of shouting and passion, and seemed endless. Every so often he raised one of his hands and pointed and waved his finger at the space in front of him.

Joy quickly became bored. She had now been standing on her high stilettos for almost half an hour. Her thick fur coat weighed her down. She did not remove it, for three reasons. The first was the church's temperature. It was freezing in there in the winter. Orthodox churches, for reasons unknown to their congregations, are designed in such a way that the sun, with its beautifully warm natural light, is kept out. Orthodoxy is afraid of the sun. If people felt the sun's warmth and beauty, instead of the gloom of the church, they might get carried away and turn back to the idolatry of the Olympian gods.

There are few if any Hellenic churches where the sun enters to warm people.

The second reason was that there was nowhere to hang her expensive coat. Draping it over her arm would be tiresome and restrict her movement every time she had to cross herself or go down on her knees. Where she stood there were no chairs or pews on which to put it.

The third reason was that, once folded, the coat couldn't be admired by the rest of the congregation. A folded fur coat loses its glory. Joy took the position that such coats must be flaunted.

Now she was completely losing patience. Today Anthony was going much too far with his verbal diarrhoea. Joy and everybody else in Portovecchio knew that his sermons were based on a confession that some poor believer had made that particular week. You had to be really gullible to confess your sins to that man. But many Portovecchians were. She tuned in again. Who was the idiot who had told him this week that he was considering divorce?

Father Anthony had begun with some reference to an old friend and how he had decided to divorce his wife in order to marry his lover. Anthony reminded everybody of God's Ten Commandments and the evil of divorce. He was shamelessly putting forth the idea that it was much better to keep both wife and mistress rather than abandoning wife and children. Wasn't this exactly what *he* was doing, after all? He was implying that God would forgive adultery–but divorce, never! The fabric of society was dependent on unbroken marriages.

He was such a bore Joy could scarcely stop herself from yawning. She regarded him with piercing eyes. He was standing erect in the pulpit, proud, wearing his colourful, gold-

Joy comes to the rescue, and trees are uprooted

trimmed holy vestments. His red hair glowed in the light of the candles. His beard was gingery, short and curly. Joy tried to imagine contact between his hairy face and the soft skin of a woman. Everyone knew he'd been shagging Fat Foni for years. No other Portovecchian woman would have him. They all knew he was mean, stubborn and bigoted.

The more deeply Father Anthony explored the evils of divorce, the more Joy's blood boiled. She started to think that meeting him at Fat Foni's wouldn't be such a good idea. She couldn't stand that woman, blatantly selling her fat, round body in front of her husband. Joy wanted nothing to do with her.

She would have to find a way to lure Anthony to her own house. But then she remembered that she had left Theodora there, with Renee. 'Come on, come on–get on with it!' she thought impatiently. If only she could force Anthony to follow her up behind the church and into the cemetery, which nobody visited in the middle of the winter. But the rain still fell outside.

Finally, with relief, Joy heard Anthony utter his last words of the service. The people in the congregation crossed themselves several times. Bells started ringing and he gave them his last few amens.

Joy waited until everyone else had gone. It didn't take long. It was almost lunchtime and everybody's thoughts of their *pastitsada*, roast chicken with roast potatoes, or roast leg of pork, made them hurry away from the church. Joy stood by the flickering candles. Her stilettos were causing excruciatingly sharp needles to shoot up through her feet. Her unbuttoned fur coat clung to her ample body.

While Joy was waiting for the service to end, in the house near the church Anthony's wife Helena was cooking.

Helena never went to church, 'because of looking after the children', she always explained. This morning, like all the others, she had got up early and tried to get her children to heed what she told them. Anthony had left for church without lifting a finger to help her, as usual. There had been no hint of the storms to come. She had lit the fire in the fireplace, changed the babies, and washed the faces of the older ones. Then she had fed them all breakfast. When they were ready, she had sent them to a room at the back of the house where they could play on rainy days. She had lit a little stove in the corner to keep them warm.

This room was where she dried her washing and kept the olive oil, the olives and her oregano, hanging from the ceiling, Anthony's fishing equipment, his baskets, her empty boxes and his holy vestments, which she refused to hang in their bedroom wardrobe, were also there. She didn't want Anthony's smelly church clothes anywhere near her, especially after he had been visiting the dying or the already dead.

After she had settled the children down to play with their toys in this storeroom-cum-playroom, Helena started cooking *sofrito*. She always cooked plenty, so they would have enough to eat for the following few days.

Helena took veal slices from the larder. She washed them and patted them with a tea towel. She placed them on a wooden board and covered them with brown paper. Then she started bashing them with a hammer to make them as flat as possible. She liked this the best, since the bashing—apart from flattening and softening the meat—also released some of the anger inside her. She dusted the slices with flour, salt and pepper and fried them in hot olive oil, which had been warming up in a big flat frying pan. When all the slices had turned a nice golden brown, she lifted them one by one and placed them on top of each other in a shallow heavy-bottomed saucepan. She then pounded six cloves of peeled garlic, which she added to cook slowly in the pan. She lowered the flame by two points and added three handfuls of finely-chopped fresh parsley, one cup of red wine vinegar and a little more salt and pepper. Stirring them together, she boiled them for few minutes and then poured them over the meat. She replaced the saucepan with the *sofrito* over the flame and cooked it for about thirty minutes, until the meat was soft and tender and the sauce thick. She boiled potatoes and mashed them; she added butter, milk, salt and pepper. Then she mixed everything together and added a handful of parmesan to the mashed potatoes.

She had also decided to cook some vegetables. The day before she had bought two bags of greens, including spinach and endive. She had cleaned and washed them and chopped them up. She had put them in a saucepan over medium heat until they shrank and became soft. Then in a pan she had fried finely-chopped onion with olive oil, and mixed in the drained, almost-pulpy vegetables. She had added a lot of red pepper, salt and more black pepper, then a little water, and cooked the greens gently until they were soft and mushy.

Joy could see Father Anthony through a slit in the curtain on the door of the icon gallery that divided the congregation from the priest's inner sanctum. His assistant had gone, leaving him to sort out his Holy Communion dishes alone. He was taking his time, since he wanted the road empty of people when he ventured out to Fat Foni's. He was careful more from habit than from sensitivity to anyone's feelings.

Joy watched him enter the vestry. He had finished with his holy dishes. As a woman, she had no right to enter this Holiest of Holies. Otherwise she would have stormed in there, pulled him by the hair and dragged him out in front of the church, where she would have spat in his face.

She felt she had waited long enough. When she saw him going to change his vestments, she decided that this was the time for the confrontation. She went for him. Her stilettos click-clacked sharply across the well-polished geometrical tiles, and echoed through the place of God. As she entered the vestry she flung off her fur coat and, forgetting its value and power for a minute, threw it on a chair. She pulled from her neck the silk scarf that Spiro had brought from China, and kicked her stilettos off her feet. She pushed her sleeves up to her elbows, as if she were ready to wash dirty clothes. Then she crossed her arms above her stomach, just below her bosom.

Father Anthony turned towards her. 'Hello Joy—what brings you to our humble little church? Congratulations on your Spiro's name day. Have you heard from him recently?'

Joy wasn't going to respond to this shameless soft-soaping. 'Yes I have, and thank you for asking,' she snapped. 'Sit down. I want to talk to you!'

Father Anthony wasn't used to people talking to him in this abrupt manner. Superstition mixed with religious sentiment made most people treat him rather courteously. He faced Joy boldly, his hazel eyes sparkling. But he was also frowning.

'What's going on?' he asked. If he was surprised by her tone, he chose to ignore it. He remained standing.

'I told you to sit down, you monster,' ordered Joy.

'What is it?' he said. This time his voice was irritated. Nevertheless, he obeyed her. He sat down on a little chair.

'I believe it's time *you* know that *I* know what you did to John. You informer! You traitor! It was *you* who went to the police and betrayed him. He had done nothing evil. He never hurt anybody. How could you?'

Anthony's eyes opened wide. After all these years, he thought, what had brought this on?

He decided to bluff. 'What? I don't know what you're talking about. You know as well as I do that he was a bloody Communist. He wanted our country to join the Reds from the Balkans and the Russian Bolsheviks. People like him were no good for us. The whole town knew that. The police only did their job.'

He said all this quickly and loudly.

Joy made it clear that she was not convinced. 'Oh yes? Would you care to come to my house and see a copy of your testimony? There is nothing, but nothing, that can be kept a secret in this world. *You* should know that, from all your church studies. What did they teach you in that brothel of a church school you attended?'

Anthony was taken aback. Rich abuse was pouring from her red, lipsticked mouth with the forthrightness of a true Portovecchian.

'You don't know that before I married Spiro I went out for a while with Dean Pappas. He was the head of the Secret Police, remember? He was sweet to me to start with, but eventually I came to hate his anti-Communist propaganda. Very similar to yours, you ugly charlatan. Soon after John was arrested, and while I was crying on Dean's shoulder about such unfairness towards my cousin, while I was begging him to do what he could to help, he admitted, between kisses and caresses, that he could do nothing. He told me there was a written testimony against John from a distinguished member of our deeply loyal and nation-loving community. It didn't take long for me to find out who it was. It was you, you over-sexed goat! You wanted him out of the way so you could get your hands on poor Zoë. Monster!'

Joy's whole face was red with rage. Anthony was frozen in his chair. He stared at her with vacant eyes; with his tongue he licked his dry lips and part of his beard. 'She knows everything,' he thought.

'I forced Dean to give me a copy of your testimony, otherwise I wouldn't have believed him. At first I told him he was just trying to put the blame on somebody else. So the next day he brought me a copy of the original document. I've got it in my drawer.'

In fact, she had no such thing. But Anthony believed her. 'He swore me to secrecy. I could never say anything, he told me. And you don't need me to tell you what they would have done to me if I had said anything. After all, John's death was inevitable. What could we do when there were such monsters in power? Church, Police, State: you're all the same. Murderers! And poor Zoë. You make me sick every time you try to console her. Your prick governs your brain. If there is a God, He should strike you dead here and now...'

Turning her head up towards the ceiling of the vestry and with half-closed eyes, Joy went on: 'Oh no God, no–don't listen to my prayers. Keep him alive. He has to make amends for his other evil deeds.'

'What are you talking about?' blustered Anthony. 'You're wrong, you silly woman. Get out!' But he knew his denials had no power over her.

'You destroyed John because you fancied his wife,' Joy hissed at him.

'I have no idea what you mean.'

'Don't talk crap! The other Portovecchians might be total idiots, but not me. You thought that nobody would ever find out that you delivered John to the police with your false accusations. You've fancied Zoë all your life. I always knew that. So did John.' Then she paused. 'And now, you idiot, you've made an innocent young girl pregnant. How far will you go?'

Anthony rose. But there was no authority left in him. This majestic woman had always been against him, he thought. Very rarely had she visited his church, even though they had been at school together with John and Zoë. He had never been able to lure her to his services, and he had never really understood why. It had occurred to him that it might have been because Joy's brother was the right hand of a very senior member of the police. How many people now knew that he, Anthony, was a traitor? Sometimes his wife told him in anger and with fear that he was obsessed with Christian and national issues. She often warned him that he would end up in a mental hospital or even prison. But what did *she* know about anything, his ugly, washed-out specimen of a wife?

Joy, on the other hand, with her imperious manner, had real power over him. Although they had been neighbours all their married lives, they had never been more than polite to one another. Her economic standing overshadowed anything that his brand of spiritual wealth could offer. He knew what she thought. She held to the idea of all non-worshippers: the conviction that priests were drones and parasites.

'You know that we know everything,' Joy went on relentlessly. 'You should never have betrayed John. You knew he never harmed anybody. You did it all in the hope of marrying Zoë. You idiot, you lecher! Now you've gone too far, Anthony.' Her voice had become even more forceful. This time, she was shouting at him.

Anthony picked up a gold candlestick from the table and placed it on the window sill. He was seething, almost blind with rage. Suddenly he turned and went for her, trying to strike her–but she was much stronger. For a fraction of a second she lost her balance, but she managed to push him away. Then she spat in his face.

'Satyr!' she yelled.

Neither of them had considered the possibility of somebody listening outside. They had presumed the church was empty, and that everyone had gone home. With an air of great moral confidence, Joy pushed Anthony away. Looking around, she saw a chair with some vestments resting on it. She threw them off and sat down, crossing her long legs in a provocative manner. She ordered him to sit down again, opposite her, and listen. When he remained standing, she ordered him a second time, loudly and firmly. It was as if he had no choice but to obey. He sat down opposite her, incapable of taking his eyes away from her beautiful crossed legs. But his eyes were full of shock, amazement and fear, not lust.

Joy rearranged her skirt in such a manner that even more leg was revealed. Anthony tried in vain to look away.

'Theodora is pregnant. You raped her in the cemetery on the night of the fiesta. She told me everything. Now what are you going to do about it? Theodora is young and poor, and her parents have been devastated by the death of Alice. You buried her, remember? Or have you forgotten? What are you going to do? Also remember: I'm going to tell. The whole of Portovecchio and well beyond will hear what you did to John. Be sure of that! One day the Hellenes will be saved from these politicians we're forced to live under, and then we'll hang you and everybody like you. Do you want the world to know right now what you really are?'

Joy was energised. She found herself pleasantly surprised that the information she had stored so long inside her head was now proving such a tremendous help. She hadn't meant to tell Anthony everything. She was basically a kind woman—a bit obsessive about her house, certainly, but without malice. But now she had finally opened her mouth there was no reason for her to slow down. And she felt she had to do something for poor Theodora. She was only a child, after all.

'Think of something fast, or I'll tell everyone about your obsession with Zoë, and your involvement all these years with the Secret Police. The Portovecchians have trusted you because they assumed God would be on their side if they stayed close to you. They're idiots, just like you. You're the biggest idiot of them all, though. You betray, you rape and you steal for your own gratification.'

For now Joy had remembered that an envelope full of money she had passed on to Anthony a few years back from her cousin in America had not found its way into the church. Anthony had told her at the time that he had distributed the money to the poor. This was a lie, because Portovecchians were too proud to accept money from anyone. They'd rather starve. Nor had Anthony bought anything for the church, as far as she could see. He must have put the money in his own pocket.

While their verbal battle raged inside, outside the storm was battering Portovecchio. Neither of them noticed.

'You're a rapist, a thief, a traitor, a windbag...' Joy shouted, her face turning an even darker shade of red.

Then someone else entered the room. Helena had been listening all along. 'Theodora will have an abortion, just as I have so many times,' she said calmly. She came into the room holding a young child in her arms and with Mamee the cat following behind. She had covered herself and the child with a sheet of thick black plastic in order to protect both of them from the storm. Her face was wet and her hair was stuck to her cheeks and forehead. The child was crying.

The cat jumped up and sat on the dry cushion of the little chair.

Anthony was flabbergasted. 'What the Hell are you doing here?' he demanded.

From its simple shade of red, Joy's face turned beetroot. Drops of perspiration ran down her face.

'I heard everything,' said Helena. 'You've never been able to keep your holy pants buttoned, have you?'

Then she turned to Joy. 'You can't imagine how many abortions I've had. He paid for them all. Just let me think. I had one after Miranda was born, then a couple after my third, Tom. If I hadn't killed Anthony's seed, we would now have twenty children to feed. He's obsessed with sex. All he can do is fornicate, over and over again. Do you think I don't know about Fat Foni?'

Then she turned back towards her husband. 'But please feel free to continue—just as long as you leave me alone.' If she hadn't been holding her child, she would have lashed out at him, just as Joy had.

Helena had finished her cooking just as the thin rain turned into the battering storm. She could hear the wind howling. Anthony must still be in the middle of his service, she had imagined, indifferently and without reverence. The storm had raged on, and the children had joined her in the spacious sitting room full of mock-Byzantine icons. As the howling of the wind continued, they all curled up near the fireplace. Mamee the cat, who was with them, was oblivious to the storm and had decided to go to sleep. She had arrived soon after being kicked out of Blossom and Tony's bed.

Helena had drawn back the curtains and seen that the rain had stopped but that the wind had strengthened. Luckily it was a holiday, so no fisherman was out at sea in his boat. Helena couldn't remember the last time such a wind had raged through Kerkyra. It was mighty, forceful and destructive.

She had kept looking out her window, up towards the church. She had heard the bells ringing for the end of the service and seen the small congregation hurriedly leaving. Was Anthony going to Fat Foni's, she wondered, or would he come home? The children needed him so badly. His best quality was that he loved his children, and was full of energy when he played with them, as he did from time to time.

Helena watched the little lane empty. The trees and bushes in the gardens were ravaged by the wind so that few leaves remained. The only trees that stood strong at this time of the year were the cypresses, old, tall and brave, growing out of the tombs in the little cemetery. They had been there since the first dead were buried. Their roots reached deep into the graves, entwining the bones of generations. Human remains fed them, year in, year out. These cypresses grew so big, so thick and so proud with this diet of human remains that no other place in Kerkyra had such beautiful trees.

The wind increased in force. Helena continued waiting for Anthony to emerge from the church door.

Then, as she watched, suddenly the wind in a tremendous gust uprooted and lifted some trees. They fell across the cemetery. Even the cypresses started bending. The howling wind was so strong and loud, it overpowered the noises from the wrenching and crashing of the trees. She could just make out the cypresses swaying, listing slowly one by one. Their roots were lifting the slabs, pulling up the gravestones.

'God Almighty,' Helena whispered to herself. She was frightened. Turning towards her children, she said: 'I must go and find your father.' She put a guard in front of the hot stove, grabbed the youngest baby, found some plastic sheeting in the storeroom and, covering them both, ran out into the storm.

She had entered the empty church dripping with water and shivering. Anthony wasn't there, but she could hear screaming and shouting from the vestry. She recognised Anthony's voice and her neighbour's. Portovecchian women were notorious for their tempers, their shouting and yelling when confronted. No other women in Hellas could shout so loudly.

Helena approached carefully and discreetly. She hesitated outside the door listening to Joy's barrage of abuse. What Helena heard was nothing new. She knew about everything except the rape. But she wasn't surprised. Recently Anthony's libido had been totally out of control.

She had entered the vestry.

'An abortion, no question about it. You will pay, Anthony—you always pay. We'll take her to my doctor. Nobody has to know, especially not her parents. She's young; she'll recover. That's the only thing to do. What is the illegitimate child of a monster and a teenage girl to do in this world? What life can it have? It must go.' Helena's style was very matter-of-fact. That's the way she'd learned to cope with her life.

Abortions in those days in Kerkyra were common. They weren't so much a method of birth control but of damage control for its young girls. For married couples, they meant economic self-preservation. The pill didn't yet exist and condoms needed both cash and planning. Few planned sex in advance in Portovecchio. Even the *morozes*, who regularly spent their afternoons with their lovers, ignored condoms, preferring spontaneity and sexual surprise. Every doctor in Kerkyra performed abortions on demand and cheaply.

'Ask Theodora to work for you for a couple of days, please,' said Helena to Joy. 'Then you and I will take her to the Old

Town to get rid of his seed. Enough is enough. There's nothing more to be said.'

Then her tone changed. 'The trees are down in the cemetery,' she said.

Her manner had become quite serene. The baby had fallen asleep, resting his angelic head on her bosom. The plastic sheeting, still wrapped round their thin bodies, dripped rainwater.

'That is what you have to do—and you'll pay the whole cost of it, you fool,' said Joy, waving her finger at Anthony. She picked up her fur coat, and put her stilettos back on. 'How can you live with him, Helena?' she asked. Her face was now less flushed.

Then she glanced out the window. She noticed the uprooted trees and the destroyed graves. 'You must go out there quickly,' she told Anthony.

In his black cassock, Anthony ran outside. Joy followed. Helena started out against the wind towards her house. Mamee chose to follow Helena.

The cemetery had been destroyed. Every grave had lost its covering slab. Crosses had been broken in half and lay lopsidedly beside the ruins. Flowers recently left on graves had blown away, entangling themselves in the cypresses. The remains of candles stuck soggily to overturned headstones. Portrait-photographs of the dead were smashed. They lay in fragments on the ground.

Anthony gazed silently around. He was cold, wet and disorientated. Joy and her rage had affected him as no other person ever had. Everything she and Helena had ordered him to do must be done.

'This is your God talking to you. You see—He's also furious with you, monster!' It was Joy, come to haunt him. 'You have betrayed God and Man.' As she turned to go back to her house, she left him alone in the cemetery.

Anthony stood with his cassock blowing in the wind. After a while, he moved slowly away, in retreat to Fat Foni's cottage.

Joy asked Emilia to let Theodora work at her house for a couple of days. Soon after the day of the storm she and Helena took Theodora with them to a clinic in the Old Town. They put a thick scarf over the girl's head and tied it firmly under her chin. They made her wear a pair of sunglasses in spite of there being no sun at all that day. They slipped off quietly, hoping that their journey would go unnoticed.

Perhaps it did; perhaps it didn't. From beginning to end the visit took only a couple of hours, including time taken to pay. The women hardly exchanged a word on their way back on the bus. By then Theodora seemed happier and wasn't wearing either the scarf or the sunglasses. She walked a few steps behind the two older women and every so often they stopped and waited for her. She was hurting a little, but a huge load had also been lifted from her little soul.

Helena left them as soon as they reached her front gate. Theodora accompanied Joy into her house. Joy gave her some hot chocolate and made her lie down. By evening she was feeling better. She returned to her own home relieved and smiling. Her mother returned her smile, but her brother Peter looked on indifferently. Her father George continued repairing his nets.

In the days that followed, Theodora remained silent, relieved that her parents had been spared her agony. She was young and resilient, and the whole experience was soon wiped from her memory.

Chapter 9

Tony's special drink means that Louisa's *balle d'enfants* ends unexpectedly

Good Queen Frederiki
Loved eating apples called Firiki

Winter 1956–57

For Louisa, Portovecchio was becoming an enchanted world open for discovery, one that was infinitely different from anything she had known until then. Renee and Maria, with their games and adventures, filled her life with happiness and helped her forget her predicament. She came to admire and appreciate her new friends, their welcoming spirit and the warmth and security of their homes.

She admired the two neighbouring families immensely for their unity, lack of conflict and absence of tension, but above all because the mother figure was constantly present, loving and in charge. Louisa had only a vague idea why the two men of the families were missing. Renee's father, Spiro, she knew worked at sea. She had overheard the adults saying that he was a Captain in the Merchant Navy. He only visited at Easter time. When he came home he brought everybody lots and lots of presents.

In spite of what might have seemed suffocating clutter to others, Renee's house, stuffed with interesting objects, fascinated Louisa. Tourist mementoes from all over the world decorated every available space. A series of commemorative plates with portraits of the entire British Royal Family was displayed on the walls of the entrance hall. A miniature Eiffel Tower, which played a can-can tune when turned upside down, stood on the top shelf of a little étagère. A shrunken withered brown head, carried away from a head-hunting expedition in the South Seas, hung from the ceiling in the master bedroom, its image reflected in a Murano wall mirror. A beautiful doll, stiff as a model with *rigor mortis*, sat permanently on Joy's sofa in the sitting room. When visitors came they admired the doll, but she also annoyed them. Her turquoise lace skirt, its frills spread out over the entire seat, made it impossible for anyone else to sit down. On the sideboard was a huge replica of an ancient Greek urn, presumably from the Parthenon's tourist kiosk. It was full of plastic roses from China.

Louisa loved every exotic object in Joy's house. But most of all she loved the dressing gown that Joy wore when she received visitors. This incredible gown was a real Japanese kimono of slightly orangey silk material, embossed with emphatic, bright yellow chrysanthemums. Here and there enormous golden circles sparkled from its texture, making Louisa blink. She could not make up her mind if they were moons or suns. A bright green obi, tied tightly round her waist, supported Joy's ample bosom. Spiro had told everyone that he had bought the kimono from a hundred-year-old geisha in Yokohama harbour. One day Louisa heard Fat Foni telling Father Anthony that geishas definitely did not live to be a hundred. Shaking her head, Fat Foni had continued in an ironic tone of voice that she was convinced the kimono was a love token given to Spiro by someone much younger than a hundred. Father Anthony agreed.

Louisa could not quite work out what had happened to Zoë's husband, Maria's father. She had overheard whispers that he was a Communist and had vanished on the small island of Lazaretto, across the bay. How was it possible to find yourself lost on such a small island? she wondered. It just did not make sense. There were whispers that the guards had shot him. They did shoot people over there, didn't they?

But the reasons for the men's absences were of no importance to Louisa. What was significant for her was that, despite their absences, no outsider had been brought in to replace them. Although she was extremely envious of Maria and Renee, she was never *jealous* of her friends. She came to love and depend on them. Her day-to-day life was becoming more fun than her previous world of daydreaming.

Louisa regularly over-fed and spoiled Mamee, who was becoming plumper, more confident and impertinent. Louisa provided her with food and in return the cat offered the little girl enough emotional warmth to nearly fill her empty heart. In years to come Portovecchio would become her point of reference, the place that would spark her imagination, where she would return whenever she had a crisis in her adult life.

By Christmas time, Theodora had fully recovered from her ordeal. Her menstrual cycle had been restored to normal; her sailor boyfriend was back, and Emilia, Zoë and Joy all took good care of her. The three women were careful not to demand too much from the girl. They also made sure that she had plenty of nutritious food to eat. Since the abortion had been kept secret from her family, Theodora had spent no time in bed.

Adelaide, George and Peter were delighted to see that whatever had been wrong with Theodora had passed. But the entire family was still missing little Alice. Adelaide kept reminding them that their Alice was not dead; she had only left them to go where life was good, peaceful and healthy. In spite of Adelaide's theories, the others still mourned Alice. They didn't share her mother's beliefs–and they missed her.

A week before Christmas, George the Impotent One, Blossom's brother, arrived in Portovecchio with his wife Elektra. It was their annual visit. They brought with them a basket filled with walnuts, almonds, dried figs, eggs, lemons, olives, onions and garlic, and a huge bottle of olive oil. All these good things had been produced by their own hard labour. Along with them travelled three live turkeys. Maria, Renee and Louisa could not believe their eyes when they saw the couple walking up the hill, carrying the enormous basket with the three birds in tow, led along on three individual pieces of strong twine.

Blossom welcomed them with great delight. She was really happy to see her George, but not so pleased, of course, to see Elektra. She pretended, however, that the couple had a special place in her heart, and immediately treated them to coffee and cakes. She assured them that she was happy in Portovecchio, and that she had everything she wanted.

George believed her, but Elektra was not fooled by Blossom's joyful face. She knew that her sister-in-law had never really liked her, and she sensed that she was not happy in her marriage. She suspected that Blossom's union was as bad as her own. But Elektra did not care as long as Blossom was out of her way. Time and again during the visit, Elektra repeated that being married was better than being alone. Blossom and George nodded in agreement. Elektra's worst fear was that, in some moment of marital despair, Blossom might return to the village—and their home.

The couple left Portovecchio before lunch. In the past Tony had made it clear that the four did not have much in common. They departed with the excuse of some business to attend to in town.

Blossom was delighted with the gifts they had brought her from the village. She opened the basket carefully. She put away the eggs and the vegetables and tied the turkeys to the plum tree in the garden. For nearly a week Louisa had a wonderful time with the three noisy birds. She fed them corn, gave them water to drink, and after school would release them from their bondage and take them for walks around the garden. Even Mamee, who had initially objected to their presence, got used to them. Perhaps the cat was more aware than the girl that the turkeys were there temporarily. They were destined to die: one at Christmas, one at New Year and one at the Epiphany.

On Christmas Eve Blossom got up early. Louisa heard her and did the same. She wanted to decorate her Christmas tree and tie a red Christmas ribbon round Mamee's neck. After Blossom had tidied up the house Louisa heard her go out into the garden. Louisa waited and waited in the dining room for her to return to give her breakfast. But Blossom was taking her time. Holding Mamee in her arms, Louisa decided to go out and see what was holding her up.

She saw Blossom crouching by the pump, hacking off the head of a turkey. The two outraged survivors cackled shrilly in alarm, raising their heads to the bright blue sky.

Mamee jumped from Louisa's arms and went straight over to the pump in the hope that some delicacy might come her way. Louisa looked sadly at the two remaining birds. She went over to stroke them. They immediately tried to peck her, but their bonds held them back. Then she called to Mamee. The cat ignored her. Feeling suddenly cold, Louisa went back inside.

That evening, Louisa, Renee and Maria visited each others' houses to sing Christmas carols, under Theodora's supervision. After collecting a few coins, they gathered in Maria's warm kitchen to count them. Zoë offered them hazelnuts, almonds and pieces of apple dipped in honey and sprinkled with walnuts and cinnamon. She gave them *kourabiedes*, shortbread biscuits covered with icing sugar, and *melomakarona*, cookies dipped and syrup and also sprinkled with walnuts and cinnamon. They had been bought from the best cake and pastry shop in town.

On Chrismas Day the three families all had *avgolemono* for lunch. Blossom cooked theirs with the eggs her brother George had brought. Zoë did not much care for eggs, so used half the usual number. Emilia told her straight out that her *avgolemono* was no good. She determined to go across the road to Joy's that afternoon and eat some of hers. Joy had the reputation for making the best *avgolemono* in the neighbourhood.

As was the custom on the first day of Christmas, families celebrated the holiday in their own houses, among their immediate relatives. It was one thing to have plenty of food to eat, but quite another to gather plenty of relatives to share it. Christmas was above all a religious feast, meaning everyone had to go to church in the morning, so complicated preparations to cater for large numbers of guests were out of the question. Bringing together too many people on the first day of Christmas could create havoc and cause family disasters. Each family usually celebrated quietly at home, eating and relaxing.

Children enjoyed all the special food but by three o'clock in the afternoon they were desperate to abandon the boring atmosphere of their homes and to run out into the street to play. The early winter dusk left them no choice but to return indoors around five. Then they would sit with their parents beside the modestly-lit Christmas tree and listen to festive programs on the radio.

In spite of the fact that she was always on her own with Renee over Christmas, Joy cooked everything as if providing for a complete family. She sent half her tasty *avgolemono* to Adelaide and George's family, who were good at cooking fish but hopeless with meat and poultry.

Just before Christmas the butcher had been given strict orders to send Joy the best lamb's head and neck he could find, as well as a piece of beef with a nice bone and marrow. He also had to deliver one of his best medium-sized turkeys. He was under orders to clean and wash everything before the delivery, since Joy detested the rigmarole of poultry preparation.

On Christmas Day she got up early, at six o'clock. She scraped some big bright orange carrots, peeled four onions, which she left whole, and cleaned a large head of celery. She inserted six cloves in each onion. Then she placed everything in a large deep saucepan. She added three bay leaves, ten peppercorns and the head of the lamb, the beef with the bone and marrow, and the wings, neck and giblets of the turkey. She added the appropriate amount of salt and covered the lot with boiling water. As it began to bubble, she was careful to remove every bit of the scum which formed on top.

While the meats were cooking she separately boiled two big mugs of short-grain rice in plenty of salted boiling water. When the rice was ready she rinsed it under the tap and left it, covered, to one side. When the meat was cooked she took it out of the stock, placed it on a big platter and covered it with a tea towel. Then she washed herself and Renee, and both of them dressed up in their best clothes and went to church.

Father Anthony, handsome as ever in his holy vestments, conducted the Christmas service in a beautiful clear voice. The church looked festive with flowers that Fat Foni had provided and arranged. The priest's children were present, but not his wife Helena. George the fisherman was there with Peter, both dressed in their best clothes. But neither Theodora nor Adelaide attended. Adelaide stayed at home because the church reminded her of Alice's funeral, and Theodora offered to stay to keep her company. Every time she saw the priest she felt ill and wanted to run away, like a frightened animal. She continued to feel like stabbing him in the heart with a knife. She wanted to rip his cassock, stuff it into his mouth, and make him eat it. Then she would drag him to the sea and drown him.

Tony also stayed at home. He despised Father Anthony. Louisa and Blossom, dressed in their finest clothes, sat in the front pew.

When church was over everyone rushed home to finish their cooking and eat Christmas lunch.

When Joy and Renee unlocked their front door they found Mamee asleep on a chair in the hall. They laughed and agreed that the cat was a welcome visitor. Renee set the table as quietly as possible to avoid waking her, but Mamee heard her moving around and opened her eyes. The cat followed the girl to the dining room, where she jumped on to Spiro's chair.

Joy lost no time after arriving home in resuming her cooking. She changed her clothes and continued making the *avgolemono*. She put the stock back on the stove and, while it was simmering, squeezed two lemons. She beat the whites of three eggs in a large bowl until they were very stiff, and beat the yolks in another dish. Slowly she added the lemon juice to the yolks, beating continually. She stirred the mixture gradually into the egg whites. She added a cup of the hot broth to the egg-lemon bowl, still beating very slowly.

She added the rinsed rice to the stock, with a handful of finely-chopped dill and another of equally finely-chopped spring onions. Then very gradually she added the egg mixture, stirring constantly in one direction. She seasoned the soup to her taste with salt and pepper, and made sure that the *avgolemono* had become piping hot. She was careful not to let the soup boil in order to prevent it from curdling, something she had learned from her mother.

When everything was ready, mother and daughter sat at the dining table, with Mamee in the seat of honour. They ate their soup, followed by the meat and the vegetables from the platter, drenched with olive oil and lemon. Joy liked her meat and vegetables with plenty of mustard, but little Renee didn't, since she found the mustard too hot. Everything was accompanied by bread, feta cheese, *lefkaditiko* salami and small juicy local black olives, which had been marinated with plenty of orange peel. They finished their meal with fresh oranges and apples.

Mamee, who was with them throughout, condescended to eat only a big chunk of lamb's neck.

On the following day, in every house, turkeys were roasted in the ovens with potatoes, oregano, lemon, salt and pepper. The stuffing was served separately. This time, Emilia's was the best.

First she fried finely-chopped onions in olive oil, and added mincemeat. After all liquids had evaporated from the pan, she sprinkled cinnamon, nutmeg, whole cloves, salt, pepper and half a cup of short-grain rice on top. She covered the lot with hot stock and let the mixture cook until the meat and rice were ready. Then she added two handfuls of sultanas and two of pine nuts. She piled everything next to the turkey and, like everybody else in Portovecchio, served the turkey with roast potatoes. She also served a finely-shredded cabbage salad with vinegar and oil. Zoë did not eat much but Maria and Emilia finished off their meal with plenty of dried figs, dates, oranges and mandarins that filled the dining room with their fragrance.

After lunch everyone set out to visit their friends and relatives. The children played indoor games together until late at night.

Now Louisa was almost happy. For the past three years she had spent Christmas with Tony as her only company. She had cried and cried because her mother was not there, with her father repeating in vain that everything would be fine again.

This year the homely Christmas atmosphere of Portovecchio, with good company within easy reach and all the neighbours visiting each other for a friendly gossip, made Louisa feel like a member of a big happy family. All the activity helped alleviate the lonely feeling inside her.

On New Year's Eve, the second turkey had its throat cut. At midnight the *vassilopita* (Royal cake) was cut, and the gold coin hidden in it was found by Blossom. Saint Basil of Caesarea brought the mid-winter presents on his sleigh. The children were made very happy. They jumped for joy when given even the tiniest wooden toy.

Soon after New Year came Epiphany. This was marked by a dip into the freezing sea to recover the silver Cross that had been thrown into the wintry waters by Father Anthony. All the young, brave men of Portovecchio competed to retrieve it. Peter was the victor that year. He dived into the freezing water as if it were his natural home, and re-emerged holding up the prize. Adelaide took it as an omen that good times were ahead for her family.

By 6 January there were no more turkeys cackling in Louisa's garden. All had vanished into people's stomachs.

Carnival and merriment came before Lent.

Life in the house above the slaughterhouse was turning out a great success. It was the perfect house by the sea, albeit an often bloody sea. Blossom was very slowly learning *the ways of the town* and even Tony was as happy as he would ever be. He started to enjoy fishing and gardening. Indeed, he became something of an expert in growing giant squash. He intended to use the pith as sponges for washing. He loved to scrub his tired feet vigorously and had read somewhere that sponges made from the inside of this huge, long vegetable were ideal for this. So he filled every bit of empty space in their garden with squash seeds, to the annoyance of the neighbours. When he immersed himself in gardening, he often forgot his plight. Sometimes he even deluded himself into thinking that one day he might wake and find the world the way he wished it to be: with Blossom gone and Poppy back by his side.

The only room of the new house that had taken time to put in order was the drawing room. Everyone called it the Salon. Even the town people knew that the house contained a Baroque room with a vast crystal chandelier, the only house in Kerkyra that possessed such an impressive object. Taking great care, Tony had cleaned it and set up the room on his own, keeping his wife away from it as much as possible. Blossom's cleaning ability and sense of *house beautiful* was rather limited, so he wasn't prepared to risk it.

Tony had decided that the Salon would be where he would display all his treasures from times past. It would be a room that would remind him of his previous marriage and vanished lifestyle.

When the Kardakis family had built the house using the profits from importing coffee for almost a century into the old Austro-Hungarian Empire, they decided to make a big show. They had returned to their mother country with bags full of gold sovereigns and a vision of a lovely house by the sea. At that time the slaughterhouse didn't exist. The spot they chose was the best in the area. It had a panoramic view and its setting was green and leafy.

When the house was complete it looked more or less like a neo-Classical villa, a small-scale Achilleion. Like the rest of the island population at that time, its owners had developed a passion for anything to do with Empress Elisabeth of Austria and her Achilleion Palace, the jewel of the island. Girls were named after Sissi and many houses displayed postcards showing the tall and elegant Empress with the tiniest waist in the world.

As if the exterior of the house was not grand enough to impress the neighbours, the Kardakis family also spent a fortune creating the Salon. When they sat in it, it reminded them of the Baroque glories of Vienna. Like most immigrants they yearned for Hellas when they lived in Vienna (where their sitting room was a Hellenic microcosm), but once back in Kerkyra, they thought only of Vienna, the city that had provided them with opportunities to make a fortune undreamed-of in their poverty-stricken mother country.

They employed renowned local artists to decorate the room. Above the marble fireplace they had painted a fantastic mural with an aloof and miserable Empress surrounded by roses and Ancient Hellenic heroes. They imported the wood for the floor from Sweden, and great care was taken to have it highly polished to make the room appear much larger than it was. In one of the walls were set four French windows leading to the front garden and looking out over the main road, the church and Father Anthony's house. On the wall facing the door leading into the main hall stood a grand fireplace of Pendeli marble. Its mantelpiece rested securely upon the heads of two chubby cherubs. They in turn rested on two short Corinthian columns. The cherubs were naked but for a little marble nappy modestly draped over the appropriate part. They had curly gilded hair and expressionless heavenly faces that looked down on the drawing room.

The mural above the fireplace added to the atmosphere. Colourful bunches of bright blooms twined around it. Flowery wooden garlands, carved in relief, and multicoloured ribbons surrounded the frames of windows and doors. Maids, nymphs and mermaids danced in front of silly satyrs and dragons breathing out little yellow flames. The artists' efforts captured the heavenly essence of the cherubs, Sissi's sadness and the eroticism of the maids, but the depiction of evil on the dragons' faces hadn't been their forte. The dragons had been painted in dark red, with curling tails and comical faces, but the flames coming out of their mouths were more like tiny wiggling tongues. The nymphs and their friends looked as if they were quite indifferent to the monsters as they frolicked in and out of the white clouds painted on all four walls and the ceiling.

The entire masterpiece of the Salon was a parody of distant Baroque religious art. It had nothing to do with the island of Kerkyra. It was a display of megalomania in the midst of the poor fishing cottages of Portovecchio.

A few years after the house was built, the municipal slaughterhouse was erected. The aristocracy could not possibly live next to a slaughterhouse, even in Portovecchio, so it was sold to the midwife. When she moved to the mainland, she rented it to desperate Tony.

Tony had fallen in love with the house the first time he saw it. The Salon made it difficult for him to resist. Although a snob by nature his limited funds forced him to ignore the clear disadvantage of its proximity to the slaughterhouse. He thought that the style of the house, with its superb central room, would give him the status his meagre finances and uncouth new wife were slowly leaching away. The Salon was the room he had always dreamed of having. In it he placed his most precious possessions, those that he hadn't exchanged for cash in his time of need when Poppy was dying.

Louisa knew nothing about art, but subconsciously she was aware that all these pictures had something to do with Catholicism and nothing to do with Orthodoxy and her country. She had visited the Duomo in the Old Town and had seen how Catholics decorated their church. The drawing room reminded her of that. Tony's furniture fitted in beautifully. His elaborate sofas and armchairs, the coffee tables he scattered with numerous silver ashtrays, his liqueur decanters on the sideboard, and the silver and crystal vases with the fresh flowers he loved to cut from the garden, were striking elements in this room. But really all he had achieved was to make his drawing room a pretentious and even grotesque place. Numerous cream-coloured crocheted doilies covered the mahogany furniture, the armchairs and sofas, undermining the Salon's high-class pretensions.

After the drawing room had been set up, Louisa started entering it as one enters a theatre, with a sense of awe and anticipation. Her eyes would fill with wonder at the paintings and the murals. She often stood in front of the fireplace, which was never lit and had been blocked with a fire-screen stencilled with a bouquet of flowers, and pretended she was warming her hands before imaginary flames. She loved to pull clothes out of her dressing-up trunk, long, full skirts and silk tops, put them on and pretend she was a queen from some remote Northern European country. She would parade around the mahogany table, waving with her little hand at an imaginary crowd, imitating the way she had seen Queen Frederiki and her daughters wave every time they passed on their afternoon drives.

When she was living in Athens, Aunt Camilla had given Louisa a little white-and-gold clock which, when wound up, played *The Blue Danube*. At the front and on the right was the clock face, and on the left a tiny three-dimensional stage surrounded by minute red curtains. In the centre a miniature ballerina stood *en pointe*. She wore a tutu made out of white tulle with a shiny pink blouse. As the music played, she rotated on a little metal skewer which ran right through her elegantly-draped body. Round and round she twirled, driven by the rotating skewer. Louisa thought this was the miracle of miracles. She loved to dance herself. She created her own steps; in her long skirts she danced like a princess in a palace.

When Poppy was alive and his practice was thriving, Tony had collected antiques. He had chosen to hoard objects reflecting an image of bourgeois seriousness. They were displayed to enhance his status. This was a clever move, because when he needed cash the antique shops snapped them up at good prices, without hesitation. Although he had sold many of them to pay his wife's medical bills, there were still quite a few left. As Louisa danced around to the music of the little clock she could see a distorted reflection of herself on the well-polished, large brass samovar which had been given pride of place in the Salon. Originally, it had been brought from Russia. Tony had been told at the auction house that it came from *Mon Repos*, the palace in Kerkyra where Prince Philip, the husband of the English Queen Elizabeth II, had been born. Tony hadn't been able to resist the connection.

On the bookcases around the room Tony had arranged leather-bound first editions of French, German and Hellenic classics. His Guy de Maupassant stories were placed on a separate shelf so he could find them quickly. Louisa wished she could read all these books in the space of one breath. She was desperate to experience the world described in these thick tomes.

Tony also collected musical instruments. There were two that stood out: a mandolin which he used to play with Poppy, and a guitar that he never played since it had two necks. These instruments hung from hooks on the wall, silent and soulless.

When the weather was bad outside, Louisa would bring Maria and Renee into the Salon. They would often pretend that they were the Royal Family. Their imagination helped them create other scenes and people too.

Every year towards the end of the winter, the residents of Kerkyra celebrate Carnival in true Venetian style. The festivities last three weeks, and it's the only time of the year that they like to remember that for four hundred years they were not actually slaves of the Serenissima, but very much part of it. For three continuous weeks they put on elaborate masks, dress up in fancy costumes and dance in the streets. In their clever disguises, they roam around, teasing one another.

Halfway through Carnival, catching the spirit of merriment in Kerkyra, Tony decided that he would organise a *balle d'enfants* to entertain Louisa and show off his unique Salon. He invited everybody, and fixed the date of the party for the afternoon of the last Sunday of Carnival.

With the help of Blossom and Louisa, he decorated the house days in advance. He bought streamers and confetti and decorated the rooms with balloons, paper flowers and masks. He asked everybody attending to come *masqué*. He ordered lots of cakes from the shop. He helped Louisa choose an outfit. When everything was ready the three of them still had two days of excited anticipation to make sure everything was in order.

On the Saturday before the party Adelaide sent Theodora to the cemetery to put some fresh flowers on Alice's grave. It was a job that she usually did herself, but on that particular afternoon she was not feeling well. But it bothered her to imagine little Alice lying there without her usual bouquet.

There was a chill in the air, so Theodora wrapped a black knitted shawl, which had belonged to her grandmother, around her head and shoulders. Adelaide handed her the bouquet she had made. It consisted of plenty of greenery and very few flowers. Because it was still winter, not much was in bloom in the garden.

Theodora walked fast towards the cemetery. She was eager to finish her task quickly, since her sailor was off-duty that night and she was going to meet him on the beach behind her father's fishing boat. She also had to go and pick up from a friend the costume she would wear next day to Louisa's party. She was going disguised as a cat.

As Theodora hurried along, the air felt damp. A delicate mist had settled for the evening. Puddles of rainwater glistened like silver. The chimneys of the houses were smoking, since the temperature was still low.

Mamee the cat had been extremely well fed that day, not only by Louisa, but also by Zoë and Joy. Father Anthony had, however, aimed a couple of kicks at her. As soon as she saw Theodora walking up the hill, she decided to follow her. Girl and cat walked together at a steady pace. Theodora talked to the cat as if she were human, and although she seemed to listen, she did not respond. She walked surely, as if she knew exactly where they were going. When Theodora went faster, the cat adopted a springy step to keep up.

The door of the cemetery was wide open. The white marble of the gravestones and the crosses, the deep green of the cypress trees, and the little flickering oil lamps on the graves made a cheerful picture. There was no trace of the damage the storm had inflicted on the cemetery before Christmas. Every stone had been replaced and the graves had been cleared of debris. The first daisies of the season had started making their appearance. When Theodora reached Alice's little grave she bent and kissed the black-and-white photograph of her sister placed under glass in the middle of the cross. Then she reached for the vase in order to change the water and to put into it the fresh flowers she had brought with her.

With a jump Mamee reached the cross and curled around it, as if it were the most comfortable cushion in the world.

Suddenly Theodora was startled by a noise behind her. She turned quickly to the cat and saw her glaring at something beyond them. A rush of fear went through Theodora's delicate body. Her heart started beating fast. There was an instant of deathly silence. Then someone started to speak.

'Theodora, don't be cross with me…' It was Father Anthony. He stood behind her, composed and calm. His tall black hat was missing and his red hair looked longer than usual. The cold breeze was blowing it away from his face. From his left hand hung a censer. With his right he held a little black book to his chest.

Theodora stared at him for a second or two, trying to comprehend what was going on. She saw the little gold cross embossed on the cover of the book. It was as if it were staring at her. In a flash she thought: 'The Devil is here, holding Jesus' cross.'

She stepped back, dropping the vase, which broke into hundreds of pieces. Flowers, both dead and fresh were scattered all over Alice's grave.

'Help!' she screamed. 'Help!' As she turned to run, her foot caught on the low railing that encircled the little grave and she fell backwards on to the marble gravestone.

The priest spoke again. 'Don't be frightened, my baby– don't be scared.' He put down his censer and book and approached her. Remembering the kicks she had received that morning and Theodora's distress in the cemetery that other time, Mamee turned wild. The cat's hair stood up like millions of needles on a pin-cushion. She was not going to let Father Anthony come anywhere near them. She arched her body, and like lightning leapt from the cross and right into the priest's face, scratching and biting. The force of her leap knocked him down, and she stayed on top of him, attacking every part of his exposed flesh that she could reach.

Her attack gave Theodora time to scramble up from the gravestone and start running. Father Anthony fought back in silence as best he could, tightening his lips and teeth so not a sound would leave his mouth.

The sunset spread across the blue sky in a thick haze. The oil lamps continued to flicker. The cypress trees swayed.

When he limped home, Anthony's face was full of blood. His cassock was stained with mud and his hands were full of scratches. Without hesitation he lied to Helena that he had fallen into the rose bush behind the church as he was trying to prune it.

His wife produced surgical spirit and plasters, but did not suggest he should have a tetanus vaccination. His children laughed at him.

The next afternoon Louisa, Tony and Blossom made their final preparations for their party. It was so warm that Tony left all the windows of the Salon open.

All morning, their guests had been eagerly anticipating the party. They were desperately curious to see the Salon; they wanted to eat as many cakes as possible; and they looked forward to enjoying the last Sunday of Carnival. Their curiosity made them arrive early. Luckily Tony, Blossom and Louisa were already all dressed up and waiting for them.

Joy arrived at the party in her kimono, with her hair done in a style she thought appropriately Japanese. Renee was dressed like a little flower girl. Maria had become Snow White. Joy thought that Theodora, who was dressed up in her cat suit, looked subdued. What was wrong with her now? Peter came as the sea-god, Poseidon. Adelaide, George, Zoë and Emilia arrived as themselves, but wearing their best dark clothes. They were all still in mourning, but had decided to come for Louisa's sake. Zoë brought them a basket of sweet oranges, freshly picked from her garden. Emilia had made and brought along Louisa's favourite custard with cinnamon.

Blossom, who had no imagination, put on her best taffeta dress and carried a stick. She explained that she was a shepherdess. She could not tell what Tony was supposed to be. He wore a colourful bow-tie with a fake moustache and an enormous carnation in his button-hole. Both of them felt proud of Louisa who was the best-dressed, a very pink nymph.

Just for this special occasion, Tony had decided to be sociable and play his mandolin. He even planned to sing for the girls to dance. Everybody already looked as if they were enjoying themselves. Joy had brought a bottle of vintage whisky that her Spiro had brought back three years before. Fat Foni brought some of her sickly, sticky cumquat.

Father Anthony produced a bottle of Holy Water. The entire company was very surprised to see him arrive with plasters on his face and hands. Politely, they enquired what had happened to him. The rose bush story then started circulating round the room. They also asked where Helena was. He explained that she had stayed at home to look after their unruly children.

All the guests sat around the Salon listening to the music that blared out of the old German radio. On funerals, name days and birthdays everybody was welcome in people's houses, the more the better. But visiting the Salon was special, a great and rare occasion. Numbers were always a good indication of the popularity of the person visited—whether alive or dead. And the neighbours had come to love pretty Louisa. In Portovecchio nobody looked at her with pity since they had not known Poppy and had no idea of the family's past, apart from some scanty details.

Most of the visitors were dressed up. Blossom's flowery taffeta dress, with its full skirt and ample length, managed to cover up her bowed legs. She had placed a velvet hair band on her head that controlled her curly, wiry black hair. Gold chains hung round her neck and a huge non-precious green-stone brooch that her brother George had given her before her wedding rested like a lump on her cleavage.

Father Anthony wore his best cassock. He had entered the room defiantly in spite of the wounds to his face. The only free seat was the one next to Fat Foni, opposite Zoë and Theodora. The priest's face was deathly pale as he stared alternately at Zoë and Theodora.

Fat Foni looked sideways at him, mad with jealousy. Joy was still worried about Theodora. Today, she looked very thin and vulnerable.

On Theodora's lap, Mamee lay, sometimes asleep, sometimes purring as the girl stroked her. That morning Louisa had whispered into her ear and invited her to the party. Louisa had already fed her with plenty of milk and biscuits and had left in the cat's little plastic dish the tail of a fish that had been fried the previous day. She had reckoned that if she had been fed she would not make a nuisance of herself during the party.

All the visitors admired the Salon. They felt privileged to have the opportunity to come and sit and chat in such surroundings. The conversation was loud and at first full of concerns about Father Anthony's wounds. Then the topic changed, and they began to gossip about the absent midwife. She had been very anti-social, they said; she'd used this 'magnificent' room to store her tools of trade and sometimes, in desperation, even as a place to bring babies into the world.

On the big round table in the centre of the room, lots of cakes were displayed. Tony had bought a double-layered chocolate cake that took pride of place. It was Louisa's favourite treat.

She could not stop admiring it. Renee and Maria could not wait to eat it.

But first little cakes were served, accompanied by gallons of orange juice and iced water from the pump. Then it was time for the big cake to be cut and handed round. Before that, Tony, with an unusually mischievous look on his face that was rare for him, winked at Blossom. She blushed and smiled back at him. Tony then announced in a loud and pompous voice that before the cake was cut, he had a surprise for them. For the first time his neighbours saw him smiling, a smile that almost made his withered face look handsome. The room simmered in anticipation. They wondered what he was up to.

Louisa was stunned. Never before had she seen Tony and Blossom showing a united face to the world. Tony beckoned to his wife to follow him. Blossom left her chair and waddled behind him over to the sideboard. She was so happy that her vast behind swayed with joy. On top of the sideboard, among all the other ornaments was a small glass barrel full of a brownish-red liquid. Still grinning, Tony abruptly ordered Blossom to get out the brandy glasses. She did so with gusto and a smile that indicated she knew exactly what Tony was doing.

'What is it? What's going on?' everyone was asking. 'Wait and see,' Blossom replied in her peasant accent, chuckling. Meanwhile the children, becoming impatient, were helping themselves to more little cakes from the display.

Blossom passed Tony the brandy glasses one by one. He turned on a tap at the front of the barrel and poured into each one about two inches of the liquid. Blossom placed the glasses on their best silver tray, and carefully offered them round. The guests raised their glasses and then cautiously drank a little.

There were immediate murmurs of appreciation. 'Mmm—this is wonderful!' 'This is perfect.' 'This is really good...' *Gulp... gulp:* they sent it all down their throats, then asked for more. And more. What was this delicious drink?

'It's my own mixture,' Tony said with pride. 'But it's top secret. All I'll tell you is that it takes three years to make.' Blossom smiled conspiratorially. She was not going to spill the beans. The truth was that Tony had only made his wonderful potion four days before. His Sarakatsanissa sister-in-law had sent them from the Zagori a demi-john full of her own *tsipouro*, the strong spirit distilled from the remains of the grapes. It could be almost half alcohol.

Initially Tony had regarded it with disdain. He hated its smell and its bitter taste. All these mountain habits that his brother had adopted infuriated him. Since he had divorced Camilla and married Elleni, Max seemed to live on meat, *xinogala* or sour milk, yoghurt, *trahana*, quince jelly and huge blobs of butter, all washed down with numerous little shots of *tsipouro*. He had easily forgotten his olive oil tradition and in the name of love eagerly changed over to Elleni's mountain dairy diet.

Max was destined to die young, Tony believed. But after thinking a bit about the dreadful drink, he had an idea. He poured two litres of *tsipouro* into a glass container. Then he added three full spoonfuls of molasses, six teaspoons of cinnamon, a couple of teaspoons of nutmeg and some cloves. He let this stand for a couple of days. On the third day he tasted it and, deciding that it wasn't sweet enough, added a soup-spoon of honey.

Then Blossom tasted it. She enjoyed it so much that she asked for a little more. After both had indulged in a further tasting of the new brew, a miracle happened: for the first time in their married lives they started giggling and even laughing. They rushed to the bedroom. They rolled on the bed, delirious with laughter, and had sex.

After that Tony did not touch the drink again. Blossom took little shots in secret and enjoyed it even more than the first time. Just before the party Tony had strained what was left of it through a sieve which he had lined with a muslin cloth. He poured the clear liquid into the glass barrel.

The neighbours congratulated him on his achievement and asked for more. Soon there *was* no more. The glass barrel was empty and the guests were full: laughing and very tipsy.

The atmosphere in the room had become extremely festive. Little songs broke out here and there. The children were running round the table laughing, while the giggling adults teased each other. Many of them were calling 'A piece of cake, a piece of cake!' They all gathered round the table.

Tony made a show of preparing to cut the first slice. In a slurred voice Father Anthony enquired if the cutting of the cake needed his blessing. Tony ignored him; under his breath he said 'Shut up'. Stumbling, Father Anthony started walking towards Theodora and Zoë.

All of a sudden, cheeky Mamee jumped from Theodora's lap and leapt on to the table. The cat had grown brave, bold and spoilt. Now nothing and nobody intimidated her. Instead of being deterred by the crowd and the noise, it attracted her.

Her big leap took everyone by surprise. They were too drunk to stop her. She went straight for the cake.

Everyone started laughing and shouting. Tony lunged forward and in an effort to restrain the cat, he managed to overturn the table. The cake fell with a thud to the floor, and broke into pieces, then into a multitude of useless crumbs. Fruit juice spilt on the upholstered chairs. The children rolled on the carpet trying to grab the bigger chunks of cake.

Blossom began to scream. As well as everything else, her best embroidered tablecloth was ruined, and Tony's precious brandy glasses lay smashed across the floor. The drunk visitors started crawling about, pretending they were clearing up.

Blossom bent down to the mess. The skirt of her dress was caught on one the legs of an overturned chair. The snowy folds of her fat thighs were revealed to everyone in the room. Tony started shouting.

Father Anthony, red-faced and flustered, ran out of the room through the French windows–but not before he'd finished off Fat Foni's drink and stuffed into his mouth one of the little cakes left on her plate. One of his sticking plasters had come adrift, and the wound was bleeding.

Louisa was the only one who remained calm. She did not care about the ruined cake. She thought everyone in the room had gone mad. She ran from the room, followed by Tony in pursuit of the cat. He was cursing Mamee, the absent midwife and the entire population of Portovecchio. He'd had enough of all of them.

By the time he and Louisa reached the garden, Mamee was nowhere to be seen. With very different intentions, father and daughter searched the garden calling to the cat, one yelling angrily, the other pleading and affectionate.

But Mamee seemed to have vanished from the face of the earth.

Inside, the party was falling apart. Blossom couldn't stop apologising to their guests for Tony's foul language and aggressive manner. The visitors retreated politely, complimenting her on the quality of his special drink. Most were too drunk to make sense of what had just happened. When Tony returned to the house, he was still fuming with anger and his cheeks were flushed. Louisa disappeared into her den and sat with her dolls. She felt as if she didn't care about anything any more.

After everyone had finally gone home, Tony locked himself in his study in the company of a bottle of ouzo. Blossom, tired and drunk, felt she couldn't care less where he spent the night. At least she'd have the entire bed to herself. Louisa went to her bed clasping her doll. She was very sad, but no tears ran down her cheeks.

The following day was Clean Monday, the beginning of Lent. By the time Louisa got up, the house was calm. Nothing indicated the previous day's disaster. Blossom had risen early to clean up. Everything had been put back in its correct place. The flowers had been thrown away; the ashtrays had been emptied. There was a strong smell of wax. Not a speck of cake remained on the bright red Turkish carpet.

Every so often Blossom chuckled, in memory of what now seemed to her hilarious events. She had closed the shutters and drawn the curtains. The room was quiet and dark. Louisa entered the room on tiptoe. When Blossom noticed her, she crept out, taking with her the broom, brushes and bucket.

Louisa pressed the light switch and the big crystal chandelier lit up. She blinked. The smiling cherubs gazed out at her from around the fireplace, and Louisa returned their stares. She thought that even after what had happened, this had been her best party ever. Her real concern was where the black-and-white cat had gone.

The room felt serene, as if part of a fairy tale. It could have been the throne room of her fantasy world, or the ballroom where Cinderella danced with her Prince. Louisa took down from the mantelpiece her magic little clock with the revolving ballerina. She wound it up, and as *The Blue Danube* filled the room, Louisa started dancing. She whirled round and round, imagining herself as Cinderella, Snow White, Rapunzel or even one of the daughters of Queen Frederiki. Then she looked up at the ceiling and thought she could be one of the daughters of Zeus, down from Olympus. At school she'd been told all about Orestes and had developed a childish passion for that hero of Hellenic mythology. She saw herself as a young goddess waiting for him. She was confident that the nymphs danced the same way as she did. One day, when she was a bit older, a young and handsome Orestes would fall in love with her. Her heart lifted as she danced, swirling round the room sometimes slowly, sometimes fast, to the tune of the clock

Halfway through a pirouette her eyes suddenly focused on the top shelf of a small étagère standing next to the fireplace. There was something missing. Its outline was clearly visible on the slightly dusty surface, proof that somebody must have removed whatever had been there before. Louisa remembered what it was. Her grandfather's silver dagger had always had pride of place on the handsome étagère. She remembered it well. It was richly decorated with silver filigree work which glittered in the sunshine or the light of the chandelier. Tony was very proud of it. Louisa loved it; it heightened the illusion of a royal, magical place, since in her imagination queens lived in palaces full of arms. She thought she remembered Queen Christina carrying a dagger in the film.

She didn't know the exact origin of the dagger. Her father had invented lots of different stories about it, skilfully embellishing the facts in order to impress others and perhaps to increase its value.

Now something was wrong: the silver dagger was missing. Louisa made an effort to continue dancing, but *The Blue Danube* was slowing down as the clockwork spring unwound. She tripped over the curved leg of the table and fell to the carpeted floor, her eyes still fixed on the place where the dagger should have been. She picked herself up, replaced the clock carefully on the mantelpiece, and ran into the kitchen, shutting the door behind her.

Her stepmother had started on the mountain of washing-up of the dishes that had survived the party. She had already sorted out the dirty linen napkins to put in the wash. She looked dishevelled now, and sad. She had dark circles under her bulging eyes. She'd slept badly. She was sure Tony had spent most of the night in his study, drinking. He hadn't reappeared.

The kitchen was suffocatingly hot, so Louisa was surprised to see the back door closed. Why hadn't Blossom opened it? Perhaps she was worried in case Mamee invaded again. Louisa knew that the cat would never be allowed to come into the house again. She remembered sharply the way Mamee had run out of the house and how she and her father had failed to find her.

She approached the door, to go into the garden. 'Don't go out– it's too early,' Blossom shouted. Louisa recoiled. She wasn't used to Blossom screaming at her. Her orders were usually delivered in a quiet manner. Nevertheless, Louisa quickly opened the door and ran out.

For a second, the sunlight blinded her. The fresh smell of a premature spring was mixed with the permanent whiff of the slaughterhouse. But there was a deadly silence all around. Louisa knew that because it was Clean Monday, there would be no killing. Since Lent was starting, meat would not be in demand for a while. Blossom followed her and tried to pull her back, but Louisa wrenched herself away and Blossom remained helplessly at the top of the steps.

Louisa ran towards her den. She hoped that Mamee would be hiding there. Suddenly she noticed her father at the bottom of the garden. He was in his blue-and-white striped pyjamas and his shoes had their laces undone. He was pumping water and washing the silver dagger, very carefully.

Louisa ran down to him. 'Dad, what are you doing?'

'Get inside!' shouted Tony. 'It's freezing out here. Go back to your room. I'm opening some sea-urchins and cleaning a couple of snappers for your mother to cook.'

Louisa didn't believe him. His hair was dishevelled and he had a wild look on his face. Traces of blood and pieces of entrails were stuck to the basin of the pump where the water was running forcefully from the tap.

The sea before them was a pale blue colour with no traces of blood. A few white clouds obscured the mountains across the water. There were no boats out. A bird flew up, its wings flapping noisily. Blossom continued to stand at the top of the steps, her arms crossed. She looked down at both of them with a sad and sulky look.

Louisa sat for a long time in her miniature armchair in her den, waiting in vain for Mamee to turn up. Sometimes she wept. At others she just stared at the ceiling, noticing the number of spiders' webs which had been spun since the den was last cleaned. She waited for what seemed like hours.

Eventually she was called for lunch. Blossom had grilled the snappers with lemon, olive oil and oregano, and served them with a salad of lettuce, spring onions, dill and lemon-based dressing. The bread on the table was still hot from the bakery: a soft moist white loaf. There were also olives on the table, a *tarama* dip and a plate full of sea-urchins with olive oil and lemon.

'You are such a lucky girl,' comforted Tony. 'I cleaned the fish for you so you don't have to eat Clean Monday food. I know how you hate it. So eat all this good food. Remember that others have to make do with octopus and ink-fish, boiled beans and lentils.' His tone was smug.

For dessert Blossom presented the unavoidable *halva* and a bowl of well-washed Firiki apples all the way from Volos. As she was bringing them out of the kitchen she sang a childish rhyme, trying to cheer Louisa up:

Good Queen Frederiki,
Loved eating apples called Firiki,
She called her baby Constantine
Costaki didn't sound so fine.

She sensed that all was not well with Louisa. The girl's eyes were sore and red and she refused to eat her lunch. Blossom and Tony consumed half the snapper and left the rest for the evening.

Chapter 10

Easter midnight soup, and a surprise

*Christ is risen from the dead,
By death He has trampled down death,
And bestowed the gift of Life
On those who lie in tombs.*

March–April 1957

Mamee seemed to have gone forever. The cat had not been seen for weeks.

Portovecchio was in hibernation. The forty days of Great Lent, with its strict food restrictions, made Louisa even sadder. Because the weather was bad, the fishermen avoided going to sea. The slaughterhouse reduced its activities by half and its workers took the opportunity of giving the building a good whitewash. March, with its cold, wet and windy days, forced the children inside.

Mamee's disappearance had devastated Louisa, but she refused to talk to anyone about how she felt. Neither Tony nor Blossom mentioned the cat. Father Anthony, whose face was healing very slowly from her scratches, began saying how relieved he was that the little beast had vanished. Now he could dispense the last rites in peace and quiet. Sometimes when out with one of his sons he would look around for her, but only to reassure himself that she had really gone for good.

Zoë too missed the cat, but her wounded heart had more important things to grieve about. Renee and Maria often wondered aloud what had happened to their friend. They would indulge in wild speculative stories that upset Louisa. Sometimes Joy half-heartedly helped the girls to search, but really just to stop them whining.

Theodora was the only one who systematically searched for the cat. When another day ended without finding her, she was always newly filled with grief. Her father insisted that Mamee had only left temporarily, because there was not much fish about. As soon as he started bringing home his catch, he told Theodora, she would turn up. 'That's what cats do. They come and go as they please.'

Weeks had now passed since Louisa's *balle d'enfants*. The fun and merriment of Carnival had become a distant memory. Tony, in spite of church regulations, insisted that his family have a week's break from fasting to replenish their strength. He rushed out to buy feta, milk and yoghurt, and tried to make Louisa consume them all within the week. The little girl needed her protein.

By April, there were signs of Spring emerging from the winter gloom. The snow on the Albanian mountains across the water was melting and running down into the sea, chilling it further. The days were gradually becoming longer and the nights shorter. As tiny leaves and blossom began to appear on the trees and in every garden flowers started to bud, the fishermen of Portovecchio began to think of putting their boats back into the water.

On the weekend before Palm Sunday, Tony decided that the family should have a nutritious meat dish of *yiaprakia* to eat. Blossom still had the last cabbage of the season in a basket under the kitchen table, but as she prepared to start cooking, she suddenly felt sick. She had been feeling nauseous for a couple of weeks. In fact, certain parts of her body had felt entirely different since Carnival.

She returned to the dining room, sat down, and asked Tony to bring her a glass of water. He grudgingly went to fetch it. When he returned, she told him that things had changed since the night he had made his special drink. Tony said: 'What things?' but did not wait to hear the answer. In an angry and mocking tone he told her not to bother with the cooking. He would cook the *yiaprakia* himself. She didn't have a clue how to cook them in any case, he went on. Last time she'd made them they were inedible. 'Go and water the garden instead,' he commanded. 'I'll cook today.'

Blossom obeyed, smiling widely as she waddled slowly towards the garden.

Tony washed his hands with cold water and prayed silently and deeply to the God in whom he did not believe: 'Dear God, let it just be some kind of sickness… nothing else!'

Then he put on a large apron and lifted the cabbage from the basket. He found a large deep saucepan and filled it with water, which he brought to the boil. He immersed the whole cabbage upside down in the water. After about ten minutes he took a long fork and a big knife, pricked the cabbage stalk and, holding it firmly in position, started cutting off and pulling away its softened leaves, one after the other. When it had become a pile of flat leaves on a platter, he washed them under the tap to cool them down and put them aside. He threw away the water and left the saucepan for Blossom to wash.

Cooking usually completely occupied his mind but today he could not stop thinking about Blossom's nausea.

He placed half a kilo of minced beef in a bowl. He added three eggs, one chopped onion, a cup of thoroughly washed short-grain rice, two handfuls of chopped-up parsley, two of fresh dill mixed with dried mint, salt, pepper and one big tablespoon of cinnamon. He mixed the meat and rice mixture well with a wooden spoon. Then, with great dexterity, he made little parcels by placing a spoonful of the mixture on to each cabbage leaf and bundling them up. He placed them tightly together inside a wide, flat, heavy-bottomed saucepan, covered them with boiling water, poured some olive oil and a big spoonful of butter on top, then added a bit more salt and pepper and cinnamon. He placed a heavy plate inside the saucepan, wide enough to completely cover the top of the *yiaprakia*. Its weight would keep the little parcels securely together, and prevent them from unwrapping during cooking. They would retain their nice firm rectangular shape.

He then placed the lid on the saucepan and let the *yiaprakia* simmer slowly. He cooked them for about an hour, for as long as it takes short-grain rice to cook properly. While this was going on, he prepared egg and lemon sauce to accompany them. First he made a white sauce with butter, flour and milk. He added to the mixture two well-beaten egg yolks and the juice of one-and-a-half lemons. He stirred this well, brought it to the boil and when the sauce was thickened, added some dill.

He called out to Blossom to set the table quickly. By this time she was feeling much better. She appeared with a huge grin on her face, announcing that after being sick a couple of times, she now felt much better.

Tony, Blossom and Louisa sat round the table to eat their meal, *yiaprakia* accompanied by feta, bread and olives. But the only one who seemed happy was Blossom. Her temporary illness had not affected her appetite in the slightest. She loaded her plate with four little parcels and managed to eat every morsel. Louisa, apparently deep in thought, hardly touched her food. Tony ate as quickly as possible and withdrew to his study.

Louisa could not stop thinking about the cat. She yearned to have her sitting comfortingly on her lap. Many times she imagined she heard her cry, but each time she was mistaken. The cat was nowhere to be seen. She thought now how Mamee would have loved a stuffed cabbage parcel. But she wasn't there. Her Mamee had gone.

Blossom knew that the little girl was grieving. She and Tony never uttered a word about the cat. They were convinced that their silence would help Louisa forget her.

In a friendly whisper Blossom said: 'Cheer up, Louisa. Life is not too bad. If you are lucky you might have a brother or sister one day.'

Louisa scarcely heard her. She got up and listlessly left the room.

She had even been having nightmares about the cat. Easter was approaching and her teacher had started preparing the children with stories of Lazarus, Palm Sunday, Passion Week, the Crucifixion and the Resurrection. Mamee would appear in Louisa's sleep with the face of Lazarus, and her father, disguised as Jesus Christ, would pull her from the drains of the pump.

At school, Louisa listened to the stories with fascination and attention. She loved them all, but the ones about Lazarus and Jesus were her favourites. When the teacher explained about Lazarus returning from the unknown and Jesus escaping from the tomb, she thought: 'Fancy Jesus managing to bring Lazarus back to life! He was so clever, He even managed to resurrect Himself. Couldn't He do the same for Mother, and for Alice, and for Maria's father? Couldn't sweet Jesus even bring back Mamee?'

On Lazarus' Saturday, the schools broke up for the Easter holiday. During the following two weeks children would have plenty of time to forget about lessons. If they were lucky the new sun might warm up the sea and then they could have the first swim of the year, before returning to classes. But most of all, they waited for Easter Sunday and the joys it brings: the roast lamb, the red eggs, the chocolate bunnies and the Easter bread.

During Passion Week, young and old are filled with anticipation. The drama of Jesus rising from the dead is the best known story in the world, and yet in Kerkyra people behave as if it is surprising, happening for the first time. They know the sequence of events by heart, and yet when the familiar story is told in church, they always listen in wonderment. The Resurrection is celebrated with fervour, fireworks, music and kisses. People's hearts are full of the Easter message of love and hope for eternal life. The Resurrection is the best ending and new beginning one can hope for.

After Palm Sunday, everyone became preoccupied with Holy Week activities. Tony and Blossom spring-cleaned the house. Sometimes Blossom felt slightly giddy, which infuriated

Tony. But everything was changing, coming alive. The wisterias in the garden were covered in flowers, the Judas trees were producing their dark purple blooms and the rosebuds were ready to burst open. To many people, however, the streets and gardens of the suburb seemed empty without the cat of Portovecchio wandering through them. Their mascot, the loved and hated black-and-white cat, had vanished.

Palm Sunday would not be the same without her leading the procession. Everyone gossiped and speculated on her fate. It was said that a car had run her over. Or maybe she'd decided to travel on her own to find the midwife. Renee even asked the captain of the ferryboat if he had seen her travelling to the mainland.

The Thursday before Good Friday was the time all the housewives dyed their eggs red. Every mother gave strict orders to her children that the enticing red eggs should not be touched until Jesus had risen, on the Sunday. Louisa was told this by Tony, who had taken the trouble to hand-paint a dozen eggs with beautiful tiny flowers. Blossom managed to crack many of the eggs she boiled and dyed in a saucepan. She didn't seem to care. These days she was finding it difficult to concentrate on her chores. Instead, she was feeling an inner warmth, a never-before-felt happiness. She was convinced that wonderful times lay ahead.

Early on Good Friday morning, Spiro, Joy's husband, arrived home. He was a tall, lean, strong man who, like many sea captains, had a pipe hanging permanently from his mouth. Fat Foni saw him first as he came up the hill carrying two heavy suitcases as if they were light as feathers. She was on her way to the church, carrying a basket full of flowers for the

Epitaphios, the funeral bier of Christ. They greeted each other jovially, sincerely pleased to meet. Charming Spiro told her that she was the most beautiful woman in Portovecchio—after his wife, of course. When he kissed her on both cheeks, her cheap, strong perfume entered his nostrils, reminding him that he had arrived home once more.

Fat Foni considered Spiro the best-looking man alive. Unfortunately he was far too good for her, and always absent. Nobody wanted a boyfriend who was never around, she told herself.

He hurried on towards his house where he could see Joy waiting for him outside their door. Renee was already running down to meet him.

Fat Foni entered the church. Her relationship with Father Anthony was at present not very satisfactory. His sexual demands had increased; he was wearing her out. She had started suspecting him of all kinds of things, but she refrained from challenging him. If her real thoughts had ever spilled out into the world, there would be terrible repercussions for many people. These days their encounters often started with her giving him wild looks and throwing ironic but vague remarks at him about his sexual prowess. A shouting match would invariably follow. Since Fat Foni was nervous about people overhearing them, she would immediately find ways to soften her arguments. As long as he knew she was not stupid, she was satisfied. She suspected that he was becoming more and more like a dirty old man—yet her poor Paul appreciated His Holiness' devout generosity. She still enjoyed the way Anthony had sex with her. Anyway, she felt it was now too late to change her ways.

Spiro had brought presents for all the children, including Louisa, whom he had never met. Joy had told him in one of her letters that a new family, of a better class than their previous neighbour, had moved in across the road, and that Renee had a new friend.

Spiro gave Louisa the most exquisite wooden pencil case with tropical birds painted on it. He told her it was from Hawai'i. She was delighted. Louisa had never seen a father who smiled as much as Spiro. He smiled and smiled. His strong teeth could constantly be seen biting down on his impressively large pipe. He did not wear a tie but a red cravat, tied stylishly around his neck. Louisa also noticed that he smelled good. She was not used to men exuding beautiful aromas, and Mr Spiro smelled wonderful.

Throughout Good Friday the sad chimes of church bells were heard all over the island. Most of the households had bought a live sheep to slaughter at home for Easter, which they fed and fattened during Passion Week. They tied a little red ribbon round its neck and attached it to the front gate. The bleating of the sheep and the tolling of the bells made Good Friday a very noisy day. The day when no-one could eat anything at all was shrinking stomachs. At dusk the Epitaphios, decorated with flowers, was carried from the church surrounded by little girls carrying baskets of flowers. As the bells continued their sad rhythm, everyone came out of their houses and stood on the side of the road. They held lighted candles as they watched the bier of Our Lord pass by.

The procession was accompanied by one of the town bands, which played the *Marcia Funebre* from Franco Faccio's opera, *Amleto*. Normally this solemn tune, poached for this occasion by Father Anthony, was the prerogative of the Old Red Band in town, which played it every year, bringing tears to people's eyes. Theodora wept the most. Her sailor boyfriend was one of the bearers of the Epitaphios. He spotted her among the crowd as the procession passed in front of her. He saw her lovely warm eyes full of tears and her damp cheeks. She was making an effort with her handkerchief to wipe away the tears. He assumed she was crying because she was moved by what had happened to Jesus, and he was proud. He winked and smiled at her.

Everyone was pleased to see Spiro again, and they all greeted him. They agreed he was a decent man–the best in Portovecchio. He had been away for a year, and was delighted to be back home. He kissed the women and joked with the men. He commented on how much the children had grown and how the women had become even more beautiful.

After the Epitaphios had passed by, people gathered in groups to discuss the latest news. Tony and Blossom were properly introduced to Spiro. Tony thought that at last he might be lucky and have an intelligent neighbour for a change, someone with whom he could discuss world affairs. Everyone was cheering up in expectation of Easter Day.

Suddenly in the candle-lit night they heard Spiro calling to them all. He was inviting his neighbours for Easter lunch in his garden, with Joy and Renee.

'Outside Kerkyra, they put the lamb on the spit on Easter day. They don't eat *avgolemono* and they don't bake the lamb in the oven the next day,' Spiro informed them.

'But surely if we do this it will give us a bad stomach after all the fasting we've been doing?' said Blossom. Tony looked sideways at her. *She always said stupid things.*

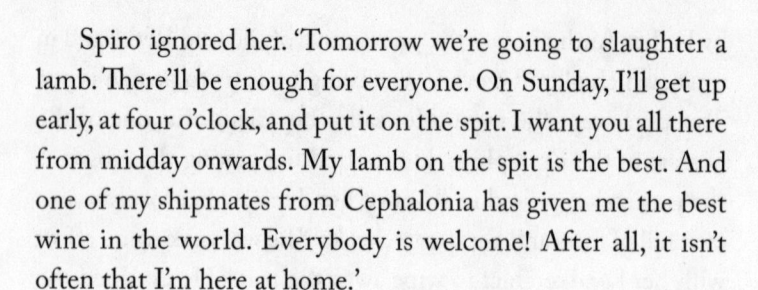

Spiro ignored her. 'Tomorrow we're going to slaughter a lamb. There'll be enough for everyone. On Sunday, I'll get up early, at four o'clock, and put it on the spit. I want you all there from midday onwards. My lamb on the spit is the best. And one of my shipmates from Cephalonia has given me the best wine in the world. Everybody is welcome! After all, it isn't often that I'm here at home.'

'Are you going to invite Father Anthony and his family?' Fat Foni asked, loudly and assertively. 'He's not here yet. The procession still has another half-hour to go.'

'Of course I want him to come—and Helena too,' said Spiro. 'I'll tell them myself. George and Adelaide—you too. It will do you good. Peter and Theodora, make sure that you bring them. But where is Theodora? I don't see her.'

Joy and Fat Foni looked round in alarm. Then they remembered, with relief, that Father Anthony was still leading the procession. Louisa was thinking that it had not been the same without Mamee out in front. But what was the use thinking about that? Her mother had gone. Alice had gone. Now the cat had gone. She tried to push away these thoughts as she ran to join her friends and play with the left-over candles.

After the procession had passed, Theodora went into her house to wash her face, dry her tears and comb her hair. Then she ran to the jetty where her sailor boyfriend had said he would meet her. She ran and ran. Away from the streets of Portovecchio the night was dark, in spite of a sky full of stars. When she arrived, panting, she sat cross-legged on the edge of the jetty and tucked her feet under her skirt. After the earlier noise, there was now a deep silence. The sea was calm and the only sound was tiny waves gently touching the posts. Far away

Easter midnight soup, and a surprise

on the horizon she could see the flickering lights of some Albanian town.

Theodora started crying again. She was missing Mamee. Where was she? She prayed no harm had come to the cat, which she loved. Mamee had been in the habit of creeping silently to her just when Theodora needed comforting. If she were still around, surely she would have come to the jetty by now.

Theodora sniffed. Then she heard something behind her that made her start. She rose.

'Boo…' It was her sailor. He took her in his arms and kissed her and felt her cheek wet with tears.

'What's going on, Theodora?'

'Mamee has gone. Our cat has gone. We'll never see her again.'

'She's only a cat,' he comforted her. 'There are lots of them round here. They often disappear, then turn up later, when they feel like it. After all, there's not much fish for them now around here.'

Theodora tried to cheer up. She asked what it had been like, being part of the procession. 'It's over, thank God,' said her sailor. 'That *thing* was so heavy.' He couldn't think of the right word. 'Now I have a sore shoulder. I hope it will get better for Easter.'

Suddenly Theodora was sobbing uncontrollably. He took her in his arms.

'Come on–I'm here… forget the cat. It's only an animal. I love you. You're the best girl in Portovecchio…'

But his kisses only made her cry more. 'What is it? Tell me.'

He took her by the hand and both of them sat on the bench at the other side of the rough little jetty.

'Now what is it? Tell me.'

Theodora took a deep breath. 'Father Anthony made me pregnant. He chases after me; he haunts me…'

'What? Father Anthony? He has a wife! As well as Fat Foni, if I'm not mistaken! What are you *talking* about?'

'He made me pregnant– on 15 August…'

'But you're not pregnant now… where is the baby?'

'I got rid of it. His wife and Signora Joy helped me. It's gone, gone out of my body.'

The boy held her tightly. She felt the rough texture of his uniform against her face, but she did not pull away.

'I love you, I love you,' she whispered through her tears.

'I love you too, my sweet girl.' He was eighteen and they had never made love.

'He tried to do it again in the cemetery when I took flowers for Alice, but Mamee scratched him and bit him. He's a monster, a monster…'

He took a handkerchief from his pocket and wiped her face. He kissed her again and again, repeating: '*I love you. I love you.*'

His kind heart, his innocence and his youth prevented him from taking in the enormity of the priest's crime. Theodora was all that mattered, and she was here, with him. Youth's natural defence mechanisms didn't allow his brain to absorb the evil that had taken place. Theodora was there *for him*. He loved her, and the baby had gone. She was still the best girl in Portovecchio.

'It's all over now, my darling. He *is* a monster. We all know that. And you know me: I love you more than anything, more than all his mumbo-jumbo. We don't need to worry about him. I'm going to marry you whatever happens in this world. I'm going to come on Sunday and ask your father to let us get engaged. Then I'll find a way to teach that monster a lesson.'

The sailor's voice was light, convincing, hopeful and full of love. Theodora stopped sobbing and withdrew from his embrace.

'What are you saying? Get engaged? I'm not a virgin any more. He touched me. He hurt me! He torments me.'

'You're all right now. I'll protect you. We're together for the rest of our lives. Think of little Alice—how pleased she'll be to see us together. Say yes, *say yes*, Theodora. Forget everyone else: the priest, Helena, Joy—and the cat. I'm here, and I'm going to make sure that everything is fine. Just say it's all right for me to come on Sunday. Soon we'll be the happiest people in the world.'

Gently he pulled her back into his arms and they kissed, it seemed a thousand times. The night was setting in, and a slight breeze made gentle waves in the water. Holding hands, they got up to leave. Theodora was still sniffling, but the boy's warm touch had started the healing process in her heart.

At eleven the following morning, pots were thrown down into the street from all the windows and balconies of Kerkyra. It was the custom on Easter Saturday. Then the bands started their joyful music and firing from the cannons at the barracks shook the town. Men hired from the slaughterhouse killed the sheep outside each house, and each gate was marked with the sign of the Cross, using a cloth dipped in the blood. The sheep-skins were stretched on cane sticks and hung out to dry.

Well before midnight, thousands of the faithful had gathered in the main square of the town, around the bandstand. Priests, led by the Bishop, all dressed in glittering brocade, gold and silver vestments, climbed up to use it as a stage. It was dimly lit: only a few street-lights illuminated the scene.

Led by the Bishop, the priests chanted the Resurrection liturgy. Exactly at midnight, the Bishop began to sing the hymn *Christos Anesti*, celebrating the risen Christ. The priests and the people in the crowd joined in. Then all the electric lights around the bandstand blazed out, church bells started ringing, and each person in the crowd lit the candle of whoever stood beside them. The square was dotted with thousands of tiny lights. From the Old Fort they could hear guns sounding a salute. Fireworks shot up into the sky, to screams of admiration and delight.

Everyone walked home still holding their lighted candles, in cupped hands. When they arrived, they made the Sign of the Cross over their doorways with the smoke.

Once inside, they ate Easter soup, *mayiritsa*, made with the liver, lungs, heart and intestines of the slaughtered lamb. Blossom didn't like this dish, because Tony washed the intestines too thoroughly, so the soup had no taste. Washing also spoiled the particular aroma of this wonderful Easter dish.

Tony had turned the intestines inside out using a long thin stick, rubbed them with salt and lemon juice, and rinsed with vinegar, 'to sterilise' them. Blossom then continued the cooking. She boiled water and put the washed liver, lungs, heart and almost disinfected intestines into it. Every so often she removed the scum that formed, and added salt. She cooked this soup for about forty-five minutes. Then she drained the meat and cut it into small pieces.

In another saucepan she fried spring onions in oil, then added the meat with lots of dill and pepper. She cooked everything for another half-hour, adding short-grain rice, well rinsed. Just before it was served, the egg and lemon mixture was added.

Louisa took one look at the soup and did not touch it. Blossom grudgingly ate a little. Tony ate the most.

On Sunday morning, nobody went to church. They had all had enough of religion. Spiro and Joy got up early to put the lamb on the spit and prepare the trimmings that went with it.

Their garden looked beautiful on this Easter Day, 21 April 1957. The wisteria covering the fence was a mass of violet blooms. The flowers in their pots smelled heavenly and the trees had all their new leaves, to provide ample shade. Most of the visitors preferred to sit in the sun, since it was still a bit chilly.

All the neighbours arrived with boxes of chocolates as presents: Tony, Blossom, Louisa, Emilia, Zoë, Maria, Father Anthony, Helena and all their children, Fat Foni, Paul, and George with his family, dressed in their best clothes. Theodora came with her sailor.

That morning at nine o'clock he had knocked on their door. He told them of his decision to get engaged to Theodora and asked for George's permission to marry her. Paul and Adelaide laughed; he was offended, but pressed on. He told them he would finish his military service in a year, and then had a guaranteed job at his father's little shipping yard. He could provide for Theodora well. Besides, they loved each other deeply. George and Adelaide exchanged glances. They thought that their family deserved a bit of happiness after all they had been through. Hadn't Peter found the Cross in the water at Epiphany? They gave their consent, smiling, and asked him to join them at Joy's and Spiro's.

Joy and Helena were delighted to hear the news, but they still thought that Theodora looked frail, pale and undernourished. Fat Foni congratulated the couple and sent wild looks towards Father Anthony, who was defiantly trying to start up a conversation with Zoë.

Tony wore a bow tie that almost strangled his neck. Blossom's expression was not particularly happy. She had started feeling quite normal since eating the *yiaprakia*, and her body was behaving as it had before she indulged in Tony's special drink. Louisa, Maria and Renee were thinking of ways to kill the boredom that Easter Sunday brings for children. They had been given enormous chocolate eggs which they couldn't wait to eat. But they had been warned to keep them until after lunch. Maria and Renee suggested that they should go to the beach and paddle in the water. Louisa listlessly agreed. She could still not get the cat out of her mind. She hoped that somebody at the party would say they had seen her, that she had definitely travelled to the mainland. But no-one did.

At around two o'clock the lamb was ready. The guests consumed enormous chunks of meat accompanied by salads, bread, feta, *lefkaditiko* salami and juicy *kokoretsi*, the entrails of the slaughtered lamb made into a huge kebab by the man who had killed it, and also cooked on the spit. At the end of the meal they all competed to break each other's red eggs. The children loved this part best. They broke many eggs. The winner was Tony, and he used his own egg to smash everybody else's. Nobody realised that his egg was wooden, a darning egg which he had painted red.

The adults all drank too much and then started talking nonsense. Father Anthony winked at Fat Foni, signalling her to join him at her house after the party.

At around five o'clock, George got up. 'Everybody, please– the weather is good and the time has come for my boat to be put back in the water again. Come, all of you, come down to the beach and help me push it in. Come on–everybody, come.'

They all laughed and started dancing to the music on the radio, telling him to wait a bit. Then after a while the entire party, still singing and dancing, left the garden and headed for the beach.

George's fishing boat, *Alice*, had been beached for the winter next to a half-ruined shed. She was covered with an enormous canvas and her oars were stacked on the roof of the shed.

'Come on, come on,' George kept shouting merrily. They all gathered round the boat. They were so glad that the fishing season was starting again. George would bring lobsters, prawns, fish, squid and all their favourite food again. Louisa looked at Tony and Blossom. Her stepmother's face was cheerful. She had momentarily forgotten her disappointment at her surprisingly good health. Tony was joking with Spiro and everyone looked happy. Louisa was puzzled. Happiness and sadness as expressed by adults were concepts difficult for her to define. Why was it that Jesus came back every year but neither her mother nor Mamee ever would? That's what she needed to make her happy.

George untied the ropes that held the canvas over the boat. They all lifted away the thick rough cover. And what did they see?

Miracle of miracles! Mamee lay at the bottom of the boat, looking up at them. Five little kittens were fast asleep around her.

Everyone started screaming. 'She's here! She's here! And she has *kittens!*' Louisa pushed to the front and leapt on to the prow of the boat. The cat jumped joyfully towards her. Louisa received her in her arms, laughing. She could not stop kissing her.

But Mamee did not remain long in the girl's arms. Without even glancing around, she ran up the hill towards the houses. Voices screamed: 'The lamb, the lamb—get the remains of the lamb…' They abandoned George and his boat and ran after her.

Theodora, her sailor, George, Adelaide and Peter stayed where they were. They lifted the kittens, one each, and, stroking them gently, took them up to their cottage. Louisa, Maria and Renee followed them, eager to find out more about these new little arrivals.

Easter Day was coming to a close. The sun had started to slide behind the mountains across the bay, and the sea was turning pink in its glow. Father Anthony and Fat Foni escaped from the beach and ran inside her house. As they rushed into the bedroom they found Mamee stretching herself on the counterpane, staring at them with eyes full of scorn and mockery.